From Messines
to Third Ypres

From Messines
to Third Ypres

A Personal Account of the
First World War on the
Western Front by a
2/5th Lancashire Fusilier

Thomas Floyd

LEONAUR

From Messines to Third Ypres
A Personal Account of the First World War on the
Western Front by a 2/5th Lancashire Fusilier
by Thomas Floyd

First published under the title
At Ypres with Best-Dunkley

Published by Leonaur Ltd

Copyright in this form © 2007 Leonaur Ltd

ISBN: 978-1-84677-144-6 (hardcover)
ISBN: 978-1-84677-140-8 (softcover)

http://www.leonaur.com

Publisher's Notes

Contents

Foreword 9
Off to the Front 13
The Prison 30
Enter Best-Dunkley 46
Millain 52
The March 57
The General's Speech 67
The Vale of Acquin 70
Back to the Salient 86
Bilge Trench 94
The Ramparts 105
Mustard Oil 111
The City and the Trenches 118
Relief 131
Watou 134
The Days Before 142
The Battle Of Ypres 148

Appendices

Murray and Allenby 178
The Infantry at Minden 181
General Rawlinson and Ostend 182
Edward III and the Order of the Garter 184
Goldfish Château 186

… Henceforth
These are our saints.

These that we touched, and kissed,
And frowned upon;
These that were frail, yet died because the good
Was overthrown.

That they in one dread hour
Were terrible
Stains not their sainthood, nor is heaven less sure
That they knew hell.

How beautiful they are,
How bright their eyes.
Their hands have grasped the key
Of Paradise!

They hold it out to us,
Our men, our sons
… To us
The lonely ones.

—Thomas Moult.

Foreword

No doubt it will be thought that some apology is necessary for thrusting upon the public all this mass of matter, relating to many persons and episodes with whom and with respect to which they may feel that they are in no way concerned. I quite realize that my action may appear strange and uncalled for to the superficial observer. But I do not hold that view. I, personally, have always felt a desire to read this kind of literature. The Press does not cease to pour forth volumes of memoirs by leading and prominent persons—matter which is all wanted for a true understanding of the history of our times. But this is not enough. We require all the personal narratives we can get; and, in my opinion, the more personal and intimate, the better. We want narratives by obscure persons: we want to know and appreciate everybody's outlook upon public events, whether that outlook be orthodox or unorthodox, conventional or unconventional. Only thus can we see the recent war in all its aspects.

The motives which have prompted me to publish this book have been well expressed by Dr. A. C. Benson in his essay on Authorship in From a College Window. In that volume there occurs the following striking passage:

"The wonderful thing to me is not that there is so much desire in the world to express our little portion of the joy, the grief, the mystery of it all, but that there is so little. I wish with all my heart that there was more instinct for personal expression; Edward Fitzgerald said that he wished that we had more lives of obscure persons; one wants to know what other people are thinking and feeling about it all; what joys they anticipate, what fears they sustain, how they regard the end and cessation of life and perception which waits for us all. The worst of it is that people are often so modest, they think that their own experience is so dull, so unromantic, so uninteresting. It is an entire mistake. If the dullest person in the world would only put down sincerely what he or she thought about his or her life, about work and love, religion and emotion, it would be a fascinating document. My only sorrow is that amateurs of whom I have spoken above will not do this; they rather turn to external and impersonal impressions, relate definite things, what they see on their travels, for instance, describing just the things which anyone can see. They tend to indulge in the melancholy labour of translation, or employ customary, familiar forms, such as the novel or the play. If only they would write diaries and publish them; compose imaginary letters; let one inside the house of self, instead of keeping one wandering in the park!"

These memoirs, then, consist mainly of extracts from my private diary and my letters home during those memorable days, spent in the Salient and its vicinity, between the Battle of Messines and the Third Battle of Ypres. The letters cover a definite period in the history of a great battalion and in the course of the war. As will speedily be noticed, the whole period was one of looking forward, practising and awaiting a great day which we all knew was not far off, but the actual date of which none of us knew until it was almost upon us. All this time our interests (and, perhaps, our fears!) were centred upon one man, the unpopular Colonel who, few of us guessed in those days, was destined to win the V.C. on "the day," going down in a blaze of glory which should ever associate his name with that battle. With that "day," which was for many of us the end of all earthly troubles and hopes and fears, or, at any rate, an end for many months, the story reaches its natural termination.

In these pages I give to the public, for what they are worth, my own personal impressions of the people and things I saw and with whom I came into contact. I hope I have revealed the late Colonel Best-Dunkley to the public just as he was— as he appeared to me and as he appeared to others. I believe that in this I am doing right. "Paint me in my true colours!" exclaimed Cromwell to Lely. That is all that any hero—and Best-Dunkley was certainly a hero—can conscientiously ask. And I am sure it was all Best-Dunkley himself would ever have asked. He was a brilliant young man, endowed with a remarkable personality. It is right that his memory should be preserved; and if his memory is to be preserved it must be the memory of the Best-Dunkley we knew.

The battalion which Best-Dunkley commanded has, since his death, achieved great things and acquired great fame under the still more brilliant leadership of his successor, Colonel Brighten; but we must never forget that it was Best-Dunkley who led it on the glorious day of Ypres and that it was the tradition which he inspired which has been one of the strongest elements of esprit de corps in the 2/5th Lancashire Fusiliers. All who served under Best-Dunkley remember the fact with a certain amount of pride, however unfavourably his personality may have impressed itself upon them at the time—for "All times are good when old!"

I am fully aware of the many imperfections of this book; but if it succeeds at all in vividly recalling to those who were in the Ypres Salient in 1917 the atmosphere of that time, and if it should encourage others to risk a similar venture, I shall feel amply rewarded.

CHAPTER 1
Off to the Front

I had been to France before—in 1916, during the Battle of the Somme—but not as an officer; in 1916 I was a private in the Royal Fusiliers, and I had received orders to return to "Blighty" in order to proceed to an officer cadet battalion at Gailes, in Ayrshire, before I had been able to see what a front-line trench was like. So this, then, was my first experience of war—my "baptism of fire." I had seen and heard those magnificent bombardments up the line in 1916, and had gazed with awestruck admiration upon the strange horizon far away from my tents at Boulogne and Étaples, wondering what it must be like to be amongst it all, and expecting to be amongst it all in the course of a day or two; but, as I have already observed, I was recalled to England, and was not destined to be amongst it until the following summer. But now, at last, the experience, the great adventure to which I had been looking forward so long, was to be mine. I was gazetted a second-lieutenant in the 5th (Territorial) Lancashire Fusiliers on March 1, 1917; on March 26, I reported for duty with the 5th (Reserve) Lancashire Fusiliers at South Camp, Ripon, where I spent some unpleasant weeks amongst snow and mud; from Ripon the unit proceeded to Scarborough, where I rejoined it after having spent a couple of weeks in hospital, with tonsillitis, at the former place. Shortly after this, I received orders to proceed overseas, and returned to my home in Middleton Junction to spend my embarkation leave.

That leave was spent in the happy way in which all such leaves were spent during the Great War, terminating with a visit to the Gaiety, in Manchester, in conjunction with my father and mother, where we saw a most enjoyable comedy entitled "The Two Miss Farndons."

I bid farewell to my parents on Victoria Station at 10.35 that evening—Friday, May 25, 1917; and I then proceeded to the train which was to carry me away to England's capital. The following letter, written at Folkestone at 11.15 the following morning, describes my journey up to that moment:

MAY 26TH. I hope you and Father got home safely last night and are not worrying. My train left Manchester at 11.20. I had to change at Stockport. In neither case could I get a carriage to myself, but I managed to doze. When dawn broke we were in Northampton. It was 6.30 when the train arrived in Euston Station. I got a taxi across London to Victoria. There was an enormous crowd of military there, bound for France. People were seeing some of them off. I could not get any breakfast there. My train left London at 7.50. The journey through Kent is really delightful, such beautiful country. I am sorry to leave dear old England; hope I shall soon be back again!

"As we passed through Shorncliffe I noticed a house in ruins. Apparently there had been an air raid. And there has indeed! There was a bad air raid here at 6.30 last night. There is a good deal of damage done in Folkestone: I have seen it while walking about the streets this morning. There have been a good many casualties.

"The weather is glorious, delightful sunshine and hot. I am now having breakfast in a cafe in Folkestone with another officer. We sail on the *Princess Clementine* at 2 this afternoon, and so will be in Boulogne about 3.30.

I landed at Boulogne at 4 that afternoon and we went straight on to Étaples the same evening. The following letter recounts my journey and arrival at that great camp upon the sand-hills

MAY 27TH, 1917. I have now, once more, safely arrived in this place, where there is nothing but sand. I expect you will already have received my communications from Folkestone. Is the news of the raid yet in the papers? I was told that there were thirty German aeroplanes and one zeppelin. Bombs were dropped on the soldiers' camp there, and a good many soldiers were killed. Apparently the operation made a big row, for it was heard across the water in the cathedral city in which we landed.

We went on board at 1.30, but the boat did not start until 2.50. It was, and still is, tremendously hot. It seems that submarines are not harassing our transport route: for the number of ships, of various kinds, crossing was considerable. It was a pleasant voyage; but as I saw the white cliffs of Folkestone receding from my ken I could not help recalling with what rapture I beheld them on my return from France last October, and expressing a faint wish that I were again returning rather than going out! But, still, one will soon get used to France again; and we can always look forward to the next return. One thing is obvious—I am here for the hottest weather; heat, if anything, will be the trouble, not cold.

The boat stood in the harbour for some time before we could land; but we eventually did so at 4. After seeing about my kit I had tea at the British Officers' Club, opposite the Gare Centrale. Then I got into the train. It should have left at 5.45, but, like all French trains, was very late in starting. It did start a little before 7. It was a train filled entirely with officers. It ambled along in the usual leisurely fashion. When we were about half-way we noticed that a good many were standing outside on the step; some had their legs hanging out of the window, others were actually on the roof! When we came to a tunnel the latter dived in through the open windows. Others got out and spoke to girls on the way, and then ran on and got back into the train. This is how travelling is carried on 'Somewhere in France'!

The scenery, beautiful as it seemed last autumn, is much more beautiful now. It is at its best: the green grass with the dandelions and daisies, the hawthorn and the trees in bloom, little villages clustering in charming woods, the sheep and the cows, and little children cheering the train, everything sparkling in the hot sunshine; such is France—and such was the Kent I left behind me—at present. As one looks upon the peaceful country-side in France to-day one can scarcely realize that war is raging in all its ferocity and barbarity so near. It seems an anomaly. The weather is more suggestive of cricket than of war.

I got here about 8.30, and went to the mess of the 23rd Infantry Base Depot. Here I found Bridgestock, Hamer, and Allin (officers who had been at Scarborough with me, and had come out a few days earlier). They have been here nearly a week. They are going to the 3/5th Lancashire Fusiliers. I had some supper before going to bed in my tent. We are three in a tent. Leigh and Macdonald are the names of my tent companions.

Fortunately it is Sunday to-day. So we did not get up until 7.45. I did not feel like rising until then!

We (the twenty Lancashire Fusilier officers who arrived here yesterday) saw the Adjutant, Captain Reid, this morning, in the orderly room, and had some information given to us. I spent most of the morning at the field cashier's, waiting for an 'advance of pay book'! Then lunch. It is now about 2.30 in the afternoon.

As I expected, I find that I have too much kit: I am told that I shall have to get rid of some when I get to my unit. I am at present writing on my nice table, but no other officers have brought out tables or chairs or anything of that kind! Well—we shall see....

MAY 28TH, 1917. It is still boiling hot; thank goodness we have finished for to-day! I must first, however, tell you how I spent the remainder of yesterday, after writing home. I spent the afternoon in the town. I explored most of it. Happening to pass the church, I saw a great crowd. It was full inside; the west doors were open, and people were sitting in the doorway and standing out in the street watching the service. So I too stopped and watched. It was most interesting, but as the service was conducted in French (apparently the Gallican Church differs from the Roman Catholic Church in England in that the service is conducted in the vernacular), I do not know what the service was. Although most of it was in French, bits were in Latin. It was exceptionally spectacular. There were about a hundred little boys in surplices and little girls in white veils (as if dressed for confirmation), all carrying long, lighted candles. Music and hymns were proceeding all the time. The little boys and girls were standing still part of the time, and processing up and down the chancel at other times. Eventually they all processed past the senior priest, attired in full vestments; and he blew out their candles as they passed. Towards the close of the service, a little girl, carrying her candle, was brought out by the priest and stationed in front of the altar with her face to the congregation; then she recited, in French, something which sounded like a very long creed. She was only about twelve or thirteen; but she did it without a stop, and in a clear, pleasant voice. After that a bell rang, everybody bent their heads, and the priest pronounced the Benediction. Then the congregation came out, and behind came the boys and girls and the priest. The people lined the road, and the procession walked on until it reached a kind of yard leading to some institute. The people followed. They all halted inside here. Then the priest prepared to make a little speech and pronounce another Benediction; but he would not proceed until all the little choir boys were perfectly quiet. He waited about five minutes. Then he preached a brief sermon (of course in French) directed to the children. I could not understand much of what he was talking about; but I think he was very eloquent. I could deduce from words here and there that he was reminding them that their fathers and brothers and uncles were fighting at the front, and telling them that if they were not good little boys and girls their fathers and brothers and uncles would fall in battle! Then he pronounced his final Benediction, and we scattered—5.20.

I could see that everybody was discussing the service and the sermon. I overheard a Frenchman in frock coat and top hat, who seemed to be a churchwarden or something of the kind, expressing his appreciation of the latter.

Then I came back to camp and paraded for a box-respirator! We then went through 'tear gas.' Then dinner. I sat at the Commandant's table. He was talking about a great concentration up North—guns and supplies and men swarming there recently....

After dinner I went to bed. Thus ended Whitsun Day, 1917.

I got up at 7.15 this morning. Breakfast. Then down to the 'bull ring' in full marching order. Gas all day. Fortunately we were under nice shady trees most of the time. We had sandwiches down there between 12 and 1, and got back at 4.30, feeling very hot after the march. Then tea....

Hamer, Bridgestock, and Allin have gone up the line this morning. I am posted to the 2/5th Lancashire

Fusiliers (the battalion Norman Kemp was in!). I shall not be going up the line for a few days, but by the time your reply to this reaches me I shall be there....

My diary of that same day, May 28, records: "To Paris Plage in the evening." And my letter written home the following day proceeds as follows:

MAY 29TH. After writing home yesterday I walked down town, and took a car to the seaside place opposite. The country through which the car went was pretty, and the seaside place quite passable; all right in peace-time I should think. Unfortunately the last car back leaves at 8.15, so I came by it....

To-day, Royal Oak Day, we have spent on the 'bull ring' again....

I have seen David Morgan (who was in the same billet with me when we were privates together in the 29th Royal Fusiliers at Oxford, in January, 1916) this evening. I managed to find the C.R.E. offices where he works. He saw me, and came out to me. I went inside. He is very cosy there, in a nice new hut. He was working at a drawing. His hours daily are from 9 in the morning until 8 in the evening; but, as I had come, he managed to get a pass to go down town with me this evening. We therefore had a walk. He looks very well with his stripe, and he seems to be having a good time. He desires to be remembered to you both. I left him at about 8. Then I had dinner at the Officers' Club, but was not struck by it....

It is now 'lights out,' so I had better stop.

MAY 30TH. We spent the day on the 'bull ring' as usual. It has been fine. We have not, I am thankful to say, had any rain at all since I landed in France on Saturday last.

This evening I have spent parading the streets of the town. I have become heartily 'fed up' with the dirty antediluvian place. Morgan actually, after nine solid months of residence here, says that he likes it and the people. I could not have imagined that there were many of the latter whose acquaintance would be particularly charming; but he speaks upon the authority of long experience!

I also wrote down the following note at that time while I was still in Étaples:

One noticeable thing to-day (May 30) has been the number of men and transport which have been passing through on the trains all day and going north, obviously coming from one part of the Front and going round this way, to avoid the observation of the Germans, to another. We are massing troops round the great city where great battles have been fought before—concentrating for a great offensive. So there will very soon be a third battle of Ypres, and I expect I shall be present on the occasion myself. It should be very exciting. In the two former battles we were on the defensive; this time we shall be on the offensive. And I must say—pessimistic as I am on all Western offensives—this idea holds forth a faint ray of hope of success. I have always held that there is only one way in which the war can be won in the West—by a flanking offensive in the North. This is not entirely the type of flanking movement I would myself recommend, but it is an attempt at the idea—and that is something. It may prove a semi-fiasco like the awful tragedies of Neuve Chapelle, Loos, the Somme, and Arras; but it might possibly turn out a success. Then it would be simply a case of *veni, vidi, vici*!

That memorandum is particularly interesting in view of the events which followed, and the story which this narrative will tell. I always held very strong-views on the conduct of the war. I was not one of those who looked upon this great bid for world power on the part, of the German

Empire as purely a campaign on the Western Front, all other campaigns in other corners of the globe being mere "side shows." I was always a firm and consistent supporter of the "East End" school of strategy. I looked upon the war as a World War and, since the decisive Battle of the Marne in September, 1914, when the German hopes of complete and crushing victory in the West were shattered (which decision was still more finally confirmed at First Ypres), as primarily a south-eastern war. I held with that great statesman and strategist, Mr. Winston Churchill, that Constantinople was "the great strategic nerve-centre of the world war." I realized that a deadlock had been reached on the Western Front, and that nothing was to be hoped from any frontal attack there; and I also realized that Germany held Constantinople and the Dardanelles—the gateway to the East. And the trend of German foreign policy and German strategy convinced me that it was in the Near East that the menace to our Empire lay. There was our most vulnerable part; while Germany held that gateway, the glamour of the East, with its possibilities of victories like those of Alexander, and an empire like that one which was the great Napoleon's early dream, would always be a great temptation to German strategists. I therefore always used to assert that "The side which holds Constantinople when peace terms come to be discussed is the side which has won the war," and I think the events of September, 1918, have proved that my view and prophecy were correct. I firmly believe that if unity of command under Marshal Foch and Sir Henry Wilson, with the following decisive victories of D'Esperey at Cerna and Allenby at Armageddon in September, 1918, bringing about the capitulation of Bulgaria and the Ottoman Empire, and the surrender of Constantinople to the Allies, had not been attained last year the war would still be in progress. And I therefore hold that it is impossible to estimate the debt which the Allies owe to those statesmen who brought about that unity of command.

21

But to return to my story. The next day was spent, as usual, on the "bull ring." On June 1, I find that I recorded the following incident:

We have been on the 'bull ring' again this morning. The weather is as hot as ever. While we were down there a German aeroplane flew right over from one end to the other—north to south. The anti-aircraft guns were firing at it the whole time, but failed to hit it. It was flying at a great height, and the shrapnel appeared to be bursting all round it. At one time it flew directly over our heads; but it did not drop any bombs! A few minutes after it had passed, bits of shrapnel fell quite near us—within four or five yards—proving how much overhead it had been. It was quite exciting, but not quite so much so as it was during those two minutes at Dover last September. Now the question which arises is: What was its object? It did not drop any bombs. Its object, therefore, must have been reconnaissance. I suppose that it came to find out what number of troops we are moving round this way to the new battlefield in the north. Even though we may move troops by so roundabout a way, the enemy is able to find out by means of aircraft. Aircraft makes manoeuvre in modern warfare intensely difficult.

That same evening orders came through for me to proceed up the line, but, as the following letter will tell, they were afterwards cancelled, owing to some mistake:

JUNE 2ND. I had a walk down town yesterday evening. Then I came back and called at the C.R.E. office to say good-bye to David Morgan. He was in—writing letters—and I stayed a few minutes; then he walked back with me part of the way. He wished me the best of luck. We both expressed a hope that the war would soon be over! 'What a life!' said Morgan.

Leigh got up before 4 this morning, as his train up

the line left soon after that. I got up at 6, and had break-fast. My kit was taken down to the New Siding Station where I had to report at 7.50. The place was, as usual, crowded with troops waiting to go up the line. There was a train full of Portuguese troops in the siding. I reported to the R.T.O. He said 'Get in officer's coach marked C, and get out at Béthune.' Then he suddenly discovered that my name was crossed out. 'I've got your name crossed off here; I don't think you are to go. You had better stand by a few minutes while I telephone and find out,' he remarked. He then telephoned to Headquarters and, after about ten minutes, the reply came through: 'Not to proceed.' There had been a mistake about the division or something. Anyhow, I was ordered to return to camp. So I told my man to take my kit back, and returned. The others went up the line. It is funny, isn't it? I am amused. I take all these changes with equal equanimity. I am quite agreeable whatever happens.... I know that whatever happens all will turn out right. I shall arrive at the right place at the right time. It is most interesting. I expect you will be pleased at the delay!

When I got back I saw the Adjutant and reported to him. He was with the padre, an Irishman who was an officer in Carson's Ulster Volunteer Force, at the time. He was amused, and the padre said 'Lucky man!' So I have had a nice easy day, writing letters and strolling about....

There are a whole crowd of Portuguese here now. A large number marched up from the station, with band playing, this morning. I find that the Portuguese troops pay more attention to saluting than do the French; I have received more salutes from Portuguese than from French; but I hear that the discipline of the Portuguese in the trenches is very bad indeed.

I notice that it is announced in the paper to-day that

a violent artillery bombardment is in progress between Ypres and the sea. There you are—that is the preliminary bombardment which always precedes a great battle in war of to-day.

JUNE 3RD. I am still here, and have heard nothing further about going up the line. The weather is still hot and fine—summer at its best. Yesterday evening I went down town as usual. When I got back I found some Portuguese officers in the mess. Everybody was talking French; it was amusing; but I soon disappeared to my tent. Macdonald left this tent some days ago; Leigh went up the line; —— took the latter's place: so now there are just —— and I in Tent 12. He returned slightly tight about 11, and talked a lot of stuff, telling me many stories of his lurid past! He seems to have been a gay undergraduate at Jesus College, Oxford, seventeen years ago; he is now thirty-eight. His home is in ——. His two children live there. He has a daughter fifteen and a son in the Cathedral choir. Yet he himself is a Quaker! And he is in the Army! He was present at the Battle of the Marne. He is a most quaint individual altogether.

He and I were censoring-letters this morning. It was amusing, but soon became boring as most of the men employed the same formula: 'Just a line to let you know that I am in the pink, hoping this finds you in the best of health as this leaves me at present, etc.'!

I went down town this afternoon and had a bath (an expensive luxury which cost me 2s.) and strawberries and cream (which cost 3s. 6d.) That just gives you an idea of prices in this God-forsaken land named France....

I also looked inside St. Michael's Church during the afternoon service. It appears to be a case of come in and go out when you please. There is one redeeming feature about the French people: they take their religion seriously, and the children are systematically taught. One can see that. The priest is a depressing-looking old chap. The service in the Gallican Church is much nicer than the service in Roman Catholic, or extreme High Anglican churches in England. There were not nearly so many candles to-day carried in procession as last Sunday. Nor was the congregation so large.

I read the Middleton Guardian correspondence to ——— in the tent when I got back. He was interested. We then argued until about 11. Macdonald, in a tent close by, called out 'Floyd, shut up!' The latter is marked 'temporary base' for a month; that is why he has not yet gone up the line. All the others who came out when I did have now gone up the line; I am the only one left behind!

JUNE 4TH. At 3.50 this afternoon I was informed that the Adjutant wished to see me; so I went to the orderly room. He informed me that I go up the line to-morrow morning. I go to the 2/5th Lancashire Fusiliers, 55th Division....

Now I am going to bed in my tent for the last time in this peaceful place, where the only reminder of the fact that war is raging is to be traced in the encamped city on the sand dunes above the town and the swarms of soldiers. The sunset is fine, the air is now a little cooler after the heat of the day, and the sea and the river calm and refreshing.

Thus ended my long wait at Étaples. The following morning (June 5) I rose at 6. Having had breakfast, I reported at the New Siding Station at 6.50. I was ordered to get into the train which was drawn up there, and get out at Hazebrouck, where I would receive further orders from the R. T. O. there. The train moved off at 7.40. As we passed Camiers we noticed an American camp there; an American waved the

Stars and Stripes as we passed. We passed through Boulogne at 9. At 1 we reached the city of St. Omer, where the great Earl Roberts had died at Field-Marshal French's G. H. Q. in 1914. All round here we noticed numerous German prisoners working along the line; and we passed many dumps of various kinds. At 2.30 we steamed into Hazebrouck. I noticed a long hospital train standing in the station, full of wounded who were being taken to the Base hospitals. Those who were in a condition to do so looked very pleased with life.

I reported to the R. T. O. in the square at Hazebrouck, and he gave me instructions to go by the next train to Poperinghe. It was a sultry day and I was glad of a drink. I managed to get one on the station. I could occasionally hear the rumble of the guns in the distance now, but very faint.

The train left Hazebrouck at 3.30 p.m. The country looked as calm and peaceful as anything. The only signs which suggested war were the German prisoners at the side of the railway and the numerous dumps. But we drew nearer to the Front. The train halted at Abeele, a village near the frontier of France and Flanders. As we stopped here for a few minutes a number of us managed to dash into an estaminet opposite the station and get a drink! From Abeele onwards the most noticeable objects were the aeroplanes which were now very numerous above us, the presence of which indicated our proximity to the war.

At 6.30 the train came to a standstill in a station which I was informed was my destination, Poperinghe. "This is the railhead for the Ypres Salient" I was told. So out I got with my kit. I was expected. There was a mess cart awaiting me at the station; and in it I jogged along to the Transport Lines which were in the vicinity of Brandhoek a mile or so further on—on the left of the road from Poperinghe to Ypres.

The transport driver told me what it was like in that part, how it had been very quiet when the 55th Division took over their positions in the Salient from the 29th Division the previous autumn, but had grown more lively every day;

how they had received a nasty gas bombardment only a few days ago, how the Boche had recently taken to shelling us furiously and systematically every night, and how there were some very hot times ahead—there was to be a raid by a battalion in our brigade that night.

It was fairly quiet when I arrived—it was a time of the day when things generally were somewhat quiet, when the guns were resting before joining in the nightly fray—so I did not immediately notice how near to the war I had come. But I was soon to realize it.

When I reached the Transport Lines I made the acquaintance of two officers of the 2/5th Lancashire Fusiliers of whom I was destined to see much in the coming months, Philip Cave Humfrey and Joseph Roake—especially Roake, as it was his good fortune to remain with the Battalion until long after the cessation of hostilities and to be with me in the 15th Lancashire Fusiliers in the Army of the Rhine. Humfrey, by a curious coincidence, turned out—though I did not know it until many months after—to be the brother-in-law of my school-friend William Lindop!

Never shall I forget that summer evening near Brandhoek. Roake, effervescing as always with droll wit, and Humfrey, with his natural cheerfulness and affability, made me at home in their little hut at once. I can well recall the scene: a tiny little wooden hut at the edge of a large field; the wall adorned by a trench map of the Ypres Salient, on which our present position was marked in pencil, and a striking group photo of the Imperial War Cabinet, taken out of an illustrated journal, in which the well-known faces of Lloyd George and Lord Curzon seemed to dominate the picture; a little table upon which Humfrey drafted a signal message to the Adjutant of the 2/5th, announcing my arrival and asking for instructions, the table upon which an excellent little dinner was almost immediately served; outside the observation balloons in a curved line, denoting the Salient, and aircraft sweeping through the skies.

It was then that I first saw what was going to be to me a very common sight during those memorable "Wipers days"—an air fight. I had not been in the little wooden hut many minutes before Roake called me out to watch a scrap between British and German aeroplanes over the Salient. We got out our field-glasses and, in the cool of a summer's evening, when any ordinary individual in "Blighty" would be relaxing from the labours of the day in cricket or in tennis, we surveyed with interest the contests between the chivalrous heroes of the air far above. It was then that I first saw a "blazing trail across the evening sky of Flanders." There were many such in the summer of 1917, though the brilliant young airman of whose death that glowing eulogy had been written now lay sleeping beneath a little wooden cross in the grave in which the Germans, paying homage to true chivalry, had laid him at Annoeullin. Who could watch those little specks rising and falling, and falling to rise no more, up there in the bright blue sky without a thrill of admiration for these "New Elizabethans" of England and Germany?

It was during tea that I realized that I was really at the war. The guns began to boom and the hut shook with the continual vibration. And then the band of the 2/5th Lancashire Fusiliers struck up some jolly tunes in the field. War and music going hand in hand, it was difficult to know whether one ought to feel jolly or sad. I think I may safely say that we felt as jolly and gay as could be; I know that the romantic aspect was the one which appealed to me most. This was the real thing, none of your home-service games.

The bombardment became more intense as the evening progressed. After dark the Transport moved off to carry rations up to the men in the line. If it is not superfluous to do so, I would wish to pay here the warmest possible tribute to those gallant Transport men who used to "carry rations on the road from Pop to Ypres." It was no picnic. The Boche knew quite well the time that vast and apparently never ending chain of traffic would be wending its nightly way from

Poperinghe to Ypres. He shelled the great high road systematically every night. Every night some of those gallant men
would go never to return. It seemed marvellous that so many
could escape the destruction which was hurled at them; but
war is full of wonders.

My diary of that night reads as follows:

As it began to get dark the bombardment became
louder and louder and the flashes more vivid. Shells
were falling at Vlamertinghe, half way between Poperinghe and Ypres, exploding with a great sound. They
were falling here yesterday!

At about 10.30 p.m. we saw the Transport set
off along the road, taking rations and supplies up to
Ypres.... Humfrey went with them. (I would have
gone up with him, but the Adjutant of the 2/5th had
sent a message by the signals saying that I could sleep
at the Transport Lines and report the following morning.) Red Cross motors were also coming back from
Ypres with wounded. Meanwhile the moon—a full
moon—steadily rose above the Front, amid the flashes
between Ypres and Messines, the bombardment sound-
ing like thunder. It was a fine scene. If only there had
been an artist there to paint it! A farm on the Switch
Road (a new road for traffic built by the British Army)
some way off got on fire. I hear that the King's, in
our Brigade, are going over the top on a raid to-night.
Our great offensive here has not yet opened, but it will
come off before very long....

To bed 11.30, the guns booming like continuous
thunder. I was awakened in the night by shells whizzing past the hut where I was sleeping.

So I was, at last, introduced to that strangest of all music—the screech of a shell: Whoo-oo-oo-oo-oo-UMP!

CHAPTER 2

The Prison

It has already been observed that the 55th (West Lancashire) Division, after a hot time on the Somme, particularly at Guillemont and Ginchy, had come up the Salient in October, 1916. So when I joined the Division it was in the 8th Corps, commanded by Sir Aylmer Hunter-Weston ("Hunter-Bunter," as I remember Best-Dunkley calling him), in Sir Herbert Plumer's Second Army. The 55th Division was responsible for the sector between Wieltje and the south of Railway Wood.

The 55th Division was commanded by Major-General Jeudwine, of whom it has been said: "No General ever was more devoted to his Division: no Division ever was more devoted to its General." The three infantry brigades in the Division were the 164th Brigade (Brigadier-General Stockwell), the 165th Brigade (Brigadier-General Boyd-Moss), and the 166th Brigade (then commanded by Brigadier-General Lewis). The 2/5th Lancashire Fusiliers, who had been commanded by Colonel Best-Dunkley—an officer who had previously been Adjutant on the Somme—since October 20, 1916, were in the 164th Brigade.

In those days a brigade consisted of four battalions. The other three battalions in the 164th Brigade were the 1/4th King's Own Royal Lancaster Regiment, commanded by Colonel Balfour, the 1/8th King's Liverpool Regiment (Liverpool Irish), commanded by Colonel Heath, and the 1/4th Loyal North Lancashire Regiment, commanded by Colonel

Hindle, who, after winning the D. S. O. and Bar, was killed at the head of his battalion at Heudecourt during the great Battle of Cambrai on November 30, 1917. When the necessity for "infiltration" brought about the reduction of the strength of brigades from four battalions to three, the Liverpool Irish were afterwards transferred to the 57th Division. But throughout the whole of the period with which this narrative deals the Liverpool Irish were still with us.

It is interesting to note the summary of the situation written by the chronicler of the 2/5th Lancashire Fusiliers in the 1917 *Lancashire Fusiliers' Annual*:

> On May 26th, the Battalion moved back to the Prison. Lieutenant-Colonel B. Best-Dunkley went on leave the same day, leaving Major Brighten in command.
>
> Then began a very memorable 17 days—Ypres was shelled heavily every day, particular attention being paid to the Prison.
>
> By night the Battalion was occupied in digging a new communication trench, Pagoda Trench. The digging was finished in two nights, but there was all the riveting to do as well. Every night the working parties have to pass through a barrage. Our casualties during this period totalled 60 or 70. The moral of the men was very high all the time. The continual shelling, paradoxical as it must seem, hardened and prepared them as much as anything for the great day which every one knew was not far off.
>
> We had our first serious gas attack on June 3rd. It was preceded by a heavy bombardment of Ypres, after which some 25,000 gas shells were put over, lasting from 10 p.m. to 4 p.m. We were fortunate in having very few casualties.

That was the position of the Battalion when I set off to join it in the Prison cells on the morning of June 5, 1917.

I rose at 10 a.m. It was a rowdy morning. The guns were

31

still unusually lively. While we were having breakfast shells were bursting three or four hundred yards away from our hut, and we could hear occasional H. E. dropping as far back as Poperinghe behind us.

The following letter which I wrote home from my cell (which I shared with three other second-lieutenants, Gilbert Verity, Bernard Priestley and H. A. Barker) in the Prison, describes my journey to Ypres:

JUNE 6, 1917. At 11 a.m. I set off up the road with another officer to the city where my unit is stationed. We got a lift in a motor as far as a town half-way. This town (Vlamertinghe) was almost entirely in ruins. There has been an ancient church there, but only the front of the tower and all the crucifixes remain. Shells were bursting all about. We sat down on a fence and waited for another lift. It was most exciting. I have not got the 'wind up' yet; I am more interested than anything else. I contemplated a famous hill on my right. Then we got on another motor. This ride was most exciting, the excitement consisting in whether we could reach the city without being blown to pieces by the shells which were exploding to front of us, to right of us, to rear of us, and to left of us! The road was cut up by shells which had exploded on it, and trees were felled across it. We jogged a good deal riding over this debris. We saw one of our batteries on the left of the road which had been smashed by a German shell. A good many of the transport horses had been killed on the road last night, but the bodies had been removed by now. We got out of the car just outside the city and walked into it. What struggles have taken place here! One could hardly realize that in pre-war days this had been a great and flourishing city. Just a few buildings remain standing, and those all in ruins; debris everywhere, shells constantly exploding everywhere. It is reckoned that the rate of casualties in this city just now is a thousand a week; military, of course—there are no civilians here; it is a battlefield where battles have been fought, where strafing is going on now, and around which a great battle is about to be fought. One battalion in our brigade went over the top on a raid last night. Our guns are even now conducting the preliminary bombardment along the line which precedes a great offensive. And the Germans are giving it us back too! My companion was very anxious that we should reach the Prison without personally encountering any shells. He told me that the corner round which we were passing was a windy one! But we got inside the Prison safe and sound, and here I now am writing this while the shells are flying and our guns stationed in the city are speaking. The top of this building is in ruins as shells are constantly hitting it, but we are down below, and we have wire-netting to catch the falling debris.

I was received by a young Major and the Adjutant, Lieutenant Andrews. I had lunch with them and the other officers in the (Headquarters) mess-room.

There let us pause for a moment. There are scenes in one's life, pleasant and otherwise, which one can never forget, which ever rest vividly in the eye of the mind. There were many such scenes during my experiences in France and Belgium; but none do I recollect more clearly, and few with more satisfaction, than this my first meal with the 2/5th Lancashire Fusiliers. Never was a subaltern given a more friendly welcome than that which Major Brighten extended to me. I was made at home at once. Padre Newman, who seemed little more than a young undergraduate with a gay and affable countenance, but with that unselfish and utterly unostentatious heroism depicted in every feature—a typical example of the kind of hero which our public schools, with all their failings, have sent forth in hundreds and thousands during the last five years—was placing jolly records on a gramophone when I entered the little cell; and the mess-waiters were preparing lunch on a table which had been erected for the purpose.

In England I had been accustomed to "battalion messes," but out here such an arrangement was very rare. "Company messes" were the thing out here. There were generally five messes in all—Headquarters and the four companies. Major Brighten at once invited me to stay for lunch at Headquarters and, when the meal was announced to be "served," told me to sit next to him. I found him extremely interesting. The conversation was most entertaining. The subject upon which his wit pivoted during a good part of the meal was the Brigadier (always an interesting topic!), his latest sayings and possible future career 'after the war'—a period which Major Brighten always declared to be in the very near future. The first thing which struck me about Major Brighten was his youth; he was only twenty-seven. I had not been accustomed to such young senior officers in England. In fact, youth seemed to be the foremost characteristic of the Battalion. Nearly all the officers were extremely young. And I learnt that Colonel Best-Dunkley himself was only twenty-seven! It was the pride of the Battalion that it was led by youth. If ever a proof were required of the truth of Disraeli's famous maxim "The youth of a nation are the trustees of posterity," it is here in the brilliant record of the 2/5th Lancashire Fusiliers. Let Mr. Alec Waugh and the League of Youth and Social Progress carefully note that, for here, surely, is a feather in their cap!

After lunch I was posted to a company—"B" Company; and I was conducted to another cell where I found my company commander, Captain H. H. Andrews, sitting up in bed, looking very happy. It was quite the thing to stay in bed until the afternoon in those days, because the nightly working parties did not get back until just before dawn. It was a day of pleasant surprises. I had already been very favourably impressed by the magnetic personalities of Major Brighten and Padre Newman; now I was ushered into the presence of another amiable military genius, Captain Andrews. I had not been in his presence two minutes before I congratulated myself on my good fortune in having "clicked" for so delightful a company commander as Captain Andrews. Though older and very different in appearance, he was another officer of the same stamp as the lovable and brilliant Major Brighten. He was an ideal company commander. One could not hope for a better either from a military or from a social point of view. He was ability, wit, and sociability combined. Those were great days.

But to continue the reproduction of the letter quoted above:

> I am attached to B Company, commanded by Captain Andrews, and I have been appointed by him to command the seventh platoon. Just before tea Captain Andrews had me in his room and gave me maps of the district and explained—with reference to the maps— the situation. He also told me the plan of campaign and explained what Haig's intentions for the whole summer offensive are and what he requires us to do; so I now know the general idea, and I also know in detail what this battalion, this company, and my own platoon have got to do—and when; but as it is all very secret information only for officers, I, unfortunately, cannot give it you. My opinion is that the general plan is good, with the exception that I do not quite appreciate the point with respect to the particular part which this battalion (and brigade) has to play in a few days; it strikes me as being rather foolish, though it may be all right.
>
> While we were having tea the Germans set up a most terrific bombardment of this prison. Shells exploded just outside the window-opening, causing quite a wind inside the room. It is going on still; shells keep striking the wall outside. There it goes—bang! And there

are our guns smashing back at them. There again—debris scattering in the quad, the other side of the door. Whizz-bang! It is extraordinary that any walls in this city can remain standing at this rate. They say that this goes on day and night. When a shell explodes the room is temporarily darkened by the cloud of smoke which rises. This is some bombardment; it is worse than the worst of thunder-storms.

I have found Verity here. He has been here some time, and is alive and in the best of health.

Well, I really must stop now; though I could go on recording every bang as it comes; there are about two explosions during every sentence which I write.

Now do not get anxious, we manage to exist through it all; and I do not see why my luck should desert me. I am on the one point on the Western Front where I had a desire to explore. There is something doing here.

And "something doing" there was, much sooner than I expected. I had reached the Prison at Ypres just in time to hear and feel the best staged battle in history—the Battle of Messines. The following letter written home on the evening of June 7, describes Messines Night:

JUNE 7TH. Since I wrote to Mother yesterday a good deal has happened. About 6.30 I attended a conference consisting of the officers and sergeants of B Company in Captain Andrew's room; and Captain Andrews explained the scheme which he had explained to me earlier on; though he did not tell them quite as much. I, of course, will not tell you what the scheme was! Then dinner. Things were much quieter now—quieter than they had been all day. A working party of the Battalion was to leave after dinner. The 2/5th Lancashire Fusiliers are the battalion in reserve to General Stockwell's brigade at present: we hang out here in the day-time, and go out on working parties in the trenches in the Salient at night. But Captain Andrews said that I need not go out with them on this occasion. So I remained behind and censored letters. While doing so my eyes began to water—about 11 to 11.30. Then the Company mess-waiter, Private Saul (Captain Andrews' batman), came in and told me that the Germans were sending over 'tear gas.' So on with my gas helmet. The gas shells were bursting outside the windows; but I thought it safe to take off my helmet after a few minutes; my eyes watered a good deal, that was all. At about midnight I went to bed.

For three hours I slept quite comfortably. At 3.15 I was awakened by a terrific row. The whole place was shaking like an earthquake; the wall was quivering; our guns were firing rapid as fast as ever they could go; every gun in the city, in fact, every gun on the British Front for miles, was pounding the enemy with shells. A man came in to say that the order was 'everybody down in the cellar.' So I threw some clothes on and went down there. There was a crowd down there. The parties which had been out working had returned, but not without casualties; there had been a few killed and wounded. At a table in the centre of the room, a lamp on it, sat Captain Andrews, in his shirt sleeves, and other officers, seriously contemplating a message which had arrived, the purport of which they were trying to understand. The man who had brought it was under arrest as a suspected spy; but after inquiries had been made at Brigade it was discovered that he was perfectly bona fide; So Major Brighten ordered him to be set free.

I found myself next to Verity, so I asked him whatever all this hubbub was about. He replied that it was the expected push on our right—'the Messines push'—taking place. The New Zealanders (and Australians, the 36th Ulster Division, the 16th South Ireland Division, the 23rd Division, and the 47th London Division) were going over the top, and this was our barrage. Captain Andrews said that this was a bombardment which our guns were conducting, double in intensity to any which we inflicted upon the enemy during the Battle of the Somme! It was a row indeed, and it continued for some time. Then dawn broke, and it had slackened. At 5.30 we came upstairs and had some refreshment in the mess; the gramophone was set going ('The Bing Boys'—'Another little drink wouldn't do us any harm'—was the precise record which was put on as soon as we entered the mess!); things were much quieter, but we were expecting the Germans to retaliate.

It was at these early morning breakfast parties in the Prison that the grim significance of the word "Gate" impressed itself upon me. "Which gate did you come in at?" was a very common question which one officer would ask another on their return from work in the trenches. "I came in by the Dixmude Gate," or "I came in by the Menin Gate," would be the reply. And some would say that they had avoided "gates" altogether and threaded their way across the open. These gates were places of evil omen. The enemy had the exact range of them, and knew when working parties would be likely to be passing them. And upon no spot was conferred a greater legacy of awe than upon the Menin Gate. It was always one of the most terrible spots in Ypres. People were killed there every day. To go past the Menin Gate was considered to be asking for it. So a terror of the Menin Gate was bred in me before I had ever seen the gruesome, stinking spot. And the Menin Gate had taken its toll on Messines Night. My letter continues:

At 6 I went to bed again. Just as I was doing so, gas shells began to burst once more, but we did not smell much; the wind could not have been very favourable to the enemy. I soon got to sleep again. We all did. In my room, apart from myself, there are Verity, Priestley, and Barker. They are in different companies from me.

We got up at midday to-day. Things are very much quieter; there are only, on an average, about one or two bangs per minute; and those are generally caused by our guns firing shells on the enemy. Very few German shells have burst here to-day since the terrible bombardment in the early hours of the morning. We lost no officers last night, but a few non-commissioned officers and men were killed and wounded while returning last night. An official message has come through that all our objectives were captured this morning.

It was on this afternoon that Major Brighten gathered all officers together for a conference in Headquarters Mess, and read out to us, in great exultation, a "secret" Special Order of the Day by Sir Douglas Haig dated, if I remember rightly, the day before Messines. I wish I had a copy of that Order in my hands now in order that I might quote it verbatim here. In the course of his Order I remember the Field-Marshal declared that another such blow as those which we had inflicted upon the enemy on the Somme, on the Anare, and at Arras would win the war! Major Brighten, with his eternal optimism, honestly believed it; and so did everybody else. Everybody was effervescing with excitement about Plumer's brilliant victory at Messines. I hold now with Mr. John Buchan, and I realized then, that "Sir Herbert Plumer had achieved what deserves to be regarded as in its own fashion a tactical masterpiece"; but, as I have already pointed out, I took a much more telescopic view of the World War than that. So, while sharing the satisfaction of the others in the Messines success, I could not endorse the ultra-optimistic view of the course of the campaign which Sir Douglas Haig had inspired. Major Brighten was beaming with delight as he read out Sir Douglas Haig's Order, and informed us that General Jeudwine and General Stockwell, with whom he had just been conversing, were equally "bucked" about it all. And he laughingly chaffed me upon my pessimism. I told him quite frankly that I did not share the general opinion.

That night only one company had to go out to work, and the company detailed was C Company; so I was not affected. In the course of a letter written the following day I wrote:

JUNE 8TH. I went to bed about 10 last night. About 2, Barker, Priestley, and Verity returned from their working parties. Priestley was very doleful; he was mournfully discussing the horrors of the war, and of his evening's experiences in particular. And it appears that there was some reason, for he had been in command of a party of eight whose mission had been to fetch back some steel helmets from the trenches. (A ruse had been played upon the Boche on Messines Night. A large number of helmets had been placed in such a position as to encourage the Boche to think that we were concentrating troops there instead of, or as well as, at Messines and Wytschaete!) They were returning, and Priestley was remarking that the Boche was very quiet just at present, when a shell burst amongst them. Four of his party were wounded and one killed; and a piece of shrapnel went right through the tube of his box-respirator, he himself escaping unhurt. A near shave! 'Well, do you think those helmets were worth the life of one man and injury to four others?' I heard him asking.

In my next letter I wrote:

JUNE 9TH. There was only one working party last night. I went to bed at 10 p.m. At 10.20 there was a terrible row on our front. A big artillery duel was going on, machine-guns were firing continuously, and flares were going up! I sat up in bed and watched it all through the prison bars. It went on for about twenty minutes! I should think it must have been a raid of some sort. Shortly after this, Priestley came to bed, and, later, Verity and Barker. We had quite a long discussion upon all kinds of topics ranging from the conduct of the war (East versus West), and the doctrine of the Apostolical Succession, to the character and policy of Winston Churchill (whom, of course, they all detest!), and the pre-war morals of civilian Ypres, concerning which Barker held very decided views. We went on arguing until dawn broke! Then we got to sleep.

I rose at 10 this morning. When I entered the mess for breakfast I was greeted by the inquiry from Captain Andrews: 'How's Palestine?' They all think that the war will end out here and in two or three months' time! They think that the next great offensive will end it. I admit that there is a great deal to be said for their theory; our plans are good, and if successful, will probably do the trick; but I am none too sanguine. We shall see. I hope they are right. Everybody does. Everybody is 'fed up' with the war; that goes without saying. I have not read a single one of the men's letters in which they do not say that. To say that, and to inform their people that they are 'in the pink' is the stock substance of their letters!

I ought now to tell you something about my platoon. To give you the names of my non-commissioned officers is surely not giving away any information which would be of use to the enemy! So I do not see why I should not do so.

As I may already have told you I am in command of No. 7 platoon. My platoon sergeant (second-in-command) is Sergeant Williams. (He was a waiter in Parker's Restaurant in St. Ann's Square, Manchester, in pre-war days). A platoon consists of four sections, each of which is commanded by a corporal. My sections are as follows: Rifle Section commanded by Lance-Corporal Tipping; Bombing Section commanded by Lance-Corporal Livesey; Lewis Gun Section commanded by Lance-Corporal Topping; and Rifle Grenade Section commanded by Corporal Baldwin. You will notice that a Lewis Gun Section is part of every platoon; I think that is sufficient answer to your question whether the fact of my attending lectures on the Lewis Gun meant that I should go into a Lewis Gun Section.

There has not been much to do to-day; nor has anything very notable happened during the day up to now. It is now 6.40 p.m. So I will close.

JUNE 10TH. Last night the whole Battalion went out on working parties; so I had command of a party. My party was detailed to repair the parapet of a communication trench just behind our front line. I set off with Sergeant Williams and a party of fourteen men of my platoon at 9.40, just as it was getting dark. We were soon in the open fields and so could see all around us the ruined buildings of the great city. Three shells fell across the path we had traversed, after we had passed the points. Fritz was just a little too late on each occasion! We went on in the dusk, amidst the flashes of booming guns and exploding shells and flares lighting up the weird ruins and ghostly country, as far as a dump (Potidje) where the remainder of the Battalion appeared to be congregated. It occurred to me what a number would have been knocked out if a shell had burst just by this dump just then! Fortunately no such thing happened. Tools were drawn here; then we proceeded on our way by platoons. The whole region was swarming with little wooden crosses where lie the thousands who have fallen on this oft-fought, long-fought, ever contending, battlefield. We threaded our way along a winding communication trench (Pagoda Trench). We passed a party in the trench with bayonets fixed—a party of one officer, Lieutenant Alexander, and thirty men of the 1/4th King's Own—waiting to go over the top for a bombing raid on a section of the enemy front line. 'Good-byee!' they laughed as we passed them. Eventually we reached the point at which we were to commence work. Flares were going up the whole time; the enemy must have seen us: the whole crowd of us all in the open by the side of the trench which was to be repaired! When a flare goes up the whole place is as light as day for a few seconds; and they were going up all round the Salient—what remains of it, one side disappeared on Thursday morning! Now and then a machine-gun would rattle a few rounds, and we would all duck down; but none of them were ranged on our party.

At 11.20 I was informed that Captain Andrews wished to see me; and, with some difficulty, I found him. He was in a trench with the other B Company officers and Sergeant-Major Hoyle. He had sent for us in order to tell us that at 11.35 we must each bring our parties into a certain trench (Oxford Road) for refuge as we knew that the bombing raid was coming off at 11.45, and we expected that the Germans would retaliate. So I brought my party into this trench at the appointed time. We were there just in time. At 11.45 our barrage—artillery, stokes-mortars and machine-guns—opened on the section of the enemy trench to be raided (Ibex Trench from Oskar Farm to The Stables) a little to our right; and as our barrage lifted, the bombers went into the enemy trench. We could hear the bombs exploding. The enemy replied by sending 'whizz-bangs' in the vicinity of the trench in which we were taking refuge. Some of them burst within a yard or two of us; but we crouched behind the parapet, and there were no casualties.

At about 12.30 this morning, when the raid was over and things had quieted, we emerged from the trench and went back to the job. Just before we got back an ugly instrument of death familiarly known amongst the boys as a 'minnie' burst about the spot where our work was. That was not encouraging! But we went back and set to again. One or two more 'minnies' burst not far from us while we were there. You should have seen us duck! And the flares continued rising and falling. We constantly heard the shells from the big guns screaming like express trains over our heads; and every now and then a machine-gun or a Lewis gun would spurt forth its bullets. We felt anything but comfortable! One man in C Company was carried away with very bad shell-shock—a 'Blighty' all right! None of us were sorry when 2 came. Major Brighten came along just before it was time to stop. 'Is that you, Floyd? How are you going on?' he inquired as he passed me. He is liked by everybody. He is awfully nice.

Major Brighten is the young Major who is temporarily in command of the Battalion while the real Commanding Officer—the notorious Colonel Best-Dunkley—is home on leave. By the way—I have not seen Colonel Best-Dunkley yet. He was away when I arrived. I am told that it is a treat in store for me! He is simply hated by everybody. His reputation as a beast is famed in 'Blighty.' I heard about him in the 5th Reserve; and Brian Kemp told me about him when we were in Harrogate. He is discussed here every day. From what I hear he is a horrible tyrant; nobody has a good word to say for him. So I am looking forward to seeing this extraordinary man. He is only twenty-seven! His greeting to Verity when he arrived a month ago was: 'Who the d—— are you?'

As soon as it was 2 a.m. we set off back. Going back is generally considered the most dangerous of all; it is then that most of the casualties occur. When we were going along one winding communication trench shells began to burst in front of us right in our course. We bent down and dashed through the hundred yards or so which these shells were sweeping as fast as we could go. It was very hot, but we did not trouble about that; that did not matter; to get safely past the shells was the important thing. We got through all right, and we managed to get all the way back to the Prison without a single casualty. I can tell you we felt very happy when we were safely inside. To think that one should look to the cells of a prison as a haven of refuge!

In Lieutenant Alexander's bombing raid five German prisoners were captured—they are in here now—and three killed. Alexander sustained no casualties whatever, and got back safely.

We had breakfast at 3 a.m. and I went to bed about 4 a.m. I rose at 12 this morning. At breakfast we learnt some very good news. To-morrow we are leaving here and going into rest billets a long way behind the line for some time. Everybody is very happy indeed about it; I think we shall have a fine time there. So you have absolutely nothing to worry about now for quite a long time...."

Things are very quiet to-day. We had our usual gas parade outside this afternoon.

Latterly all the men have been walking about with a windy expression on their faces; now everybody looks gay in anticipation of the time in front of us. Don't you think I am really exceedingly lucky? I do.

CHAPTER 3

Enter Best-Dunkley

The following letter, written at Millain, recounts my first impressions of Colonel Best-Dunkley:

JUNE 12TH. We are now in rest billets a long way behind the line. I write to narrate to you the journey.

On Sunday (June 10) I went to bed about 10 p.m., and had only been in bed half an hour when a very intense battle appeared to have broken out on our right. A violent artillery duel was in progress, with the usual accompaniments. The thunder of the guns continued for quite a long time. I think there must have been something big on: either a further advance of Plumer's Army or a counter-attack by the Crown Prince Rupprecht. It was a big row.

Apropos of Sir Herbert Plumer, the victor of Messines: we were in his Second Army until that battle; now we have been transferred to Sir Hubert Gough's Fifth Army. I was amused when I heard Priestley telling his servant that we had moved into General Gough's Army; the servant replied 'Oh, he's a fighting man, isn't he, sir? We're in for something big now!' (General Gough had the reputation of being 'a fire eater.')

Reveille went at 5.30 yesterday morning. We had breakfast in bed at 6. It was arranged by Major Brighten that the Battalion should leave the city by platoons, each platoon moving off at five minutes interval from the ones in front and behind of it. I moved off with the seventh platoon at 8.10. We marched through the city as happily as if we were a Sunday School trip, looking at the magnificent ruins as we passed. Scarcely a gun was fired on either side the whole time. Things were extraordinarily quiet. On any ordinary occasion we would have been observed by the enemy aircraft and strafed like ——; but fortunately it was very dull at the time, the clouds precluding observation. The weather was in our favour. The whole Battalion got safely away without a single casualty! An astonishing feat. Major Brighten has reason to feel very pleased with himself. We marched along the road for a distance of about four miles, and then halted and concentrated; then we marched on together and at 10 a.m. reached the transport camp where I first appeared last Tuesday evening. Here the Battalion was halted and left to have lunch. The officers were allowed to go into the town (Poperinghe) and have lunch there if they wished. Donald Allen, the commander of the fifth platoon, and I, got lifts on two motors down to the town. Then we had baths at the Divisional Baths there. We then set off to the Officers' Club for lunch; but just before we got there two other officers called out to us from the opposite side of the road. They inquired whether we were going to the Club; and when we replied that we were, they exclaimed: 'Don't; the C. O.'s there!'

'Who? The C. O.—Colonel Best-Dunkley?' we asked.

'Yes,' was the reply. So we jolly well did not go; we went to a restaurant instead! Apparently Colonel Best-Dunkley had now returned. Everybody was very fed up at his return.

At 2 we turned up at the station. The news of the Commanding Officer's return had already spread throughout the Battalion. We got our platoons en-

47

trained, and then proceeded to the officers' carriages. It was rumoured that Colonel Best-Dunkley was going to travel by a particular carriage. You should have seen how that carriage was boycotted! Nobody would go into it. They preferred to crowd out the other carriages and leave the tainted carriage empty. It was most noticeable. I do not think there is a single person in the Battalion who would not rather travel with the devil incarnate than with Colonel Best-Dunkley.

He appeared on the scene shortly. There was a flutter of low mutterings as he appeared. I was very interested to see this extraordinary man of whom I had heard so much. He stopped two or three doors away from our own and stood talking to someone inside the carriage. He is small, clean-shaven, with a crooked nose and a noticeable blink. He looks harmless enough; but I noticed something about his eyes which did not look exactly pleasant. He looks more than twenty-seven. When war broke out he was a lieutenant. It is interesting to note that he was educated at a military school in Germany! (And he had travelled a good deal in the Far East. 'When I was in China' was one of his favourite topics of conversation.) I have not yet spoken to the man, so I am not yet in a position to judge him myself. I will tell you my own opinion of him when I have had a little experience of him. I may just remark that an officer observed in the mess this morning that he supposed that there were some people who liked the Kaiser, but he was sure that there was not a single soul who liked Best-Dunkley! That is rather strong.

Well our train moved off at about 3 p.m. We travelled through pleasant country to a little town which I cannot, of course, name. (Esquelbeck.) Here we had tea. I may mention that this place was just over the frontier—that is to say 'Somewhere in France.'

Refreshed by our tea (for the preparation of which

48

Padre Newman was mainly responsible), we began our long march at 7.15 in the evening. We marched to a village ten miles away (to Millain via Zeggers, Erkelsbrugge, Bollezeele, and Merekeghem). Colonel Best-Dunkley had gone on by himself; he left Major Brighten to carry on for the remainder of the journey. We had the band with us. I enjoyed the march immensely. It was a beautiful evening and the pretty villages through which we marched looked at their best. One thing which I have particularly noticed in France and Belgium is this: that a village, however small, seems to possess a large and magnificent church. I have not seen a single village in Belgium or France where the church is not the most prominent object. And I think that the villages are much healthier and prettier, and in every way much more inviting, than the towns. It is in such a village with such a church in pretty rural surroundings that I am now stationed. Darkness fell while we were on the march. We got here about 10.30, feeling considerably tired and ready for bed. Talbot Dickinson had been here a day or two and had arranged about billets. So the men were immediately shown into their billets. I am billeted in a farm-house; I have a nice little bedroom all to myself, and sleep in a civilian bed. So I am very well off. What do you say? I have nothing to grumble about as regards my quarters. B Company is billeted in the two barns belonging to this farm: two platoons in each barn. The Company parade in a delightful field the other side of the barns. There are three officers' messes: Headquarters and two of two combined companies. B and A Companies mess together in a house about two minutes' walk from this farm. Battalion Orderly Room is in a house about five minutes' walk from here. The other companies are in other parts of the village. General Stockwell and the remainder of the Brigade have not yet arrived, but they will be following on shortly. I am very happy here. The weather has been delightful, and the country looks fine. The trees here are very tall indeed. There was a heavy downpour of rain at tea-time: the first real rain we have had while I have been in France this time.

We have spent the day 'under company arrangements': a series of inspections in the field outside the barn.

At 5.30 Colonel Best-Dunkley wished to see all officers and sergeant-majors at Headquarters Mess. When we got there we adjourned to Battalion Orderly Room. He kept us until after 7, discussing various matters of routine. He seemed to have set his mind on purchasing a new band which was to cost £100 and for which officers should pay their share according to rank—subalterns to pay £2 each. But there was not a single person in favour of the idea! The proposal was received in cold silence. (Everybody had agreed before the conference upon the attitude to be taken up! I thought the whole affair a huge joke. Plots and intrigues always appeal to me as exciting.) Then Captain Mordecai—O.C. C Company—said that he did not think it worth it 'Since the war is nearly over.' The Colonel did not like that idea at all! He appealed to Major Brighten for his opinion; and Major Brighten urged that if we are to spend money like this it would be better spent in helping the men in some way. Others pointed out that one band was sufficient, and said that they would rather pay 10s. each for the improvement of the present band. Colonel Best-Dunkley blinked and twitched his nose in a disapproving manner. Eventually it was decided that we should not get a new band, but that we should all pay 10s. towards the present band. Colonel Best-Dunkley had set his mind on this band enterprise; I do not suppose he is at all pleased that it has not been taken up! The officers are all congratulating themselves on their victory. Colonel Best-Dunkley has announced that we must all see that the men have their equipment blancoed and polished until it sparkles. I have no personal quarrel with Colonel Best-Dunkley myself yet—in fact I have not yet exchanged a word with him—but I cannot say that I am very favourably impressed.

CHAPTER 4

Millain

It was at Millain that I had my first personal interview
with Colonel Best-Dunkley. That interview is recounted in
the following letter:

> JUNE 13TH. The weather continues to be glorious:
> too hot to do anything. I am Orderly Officer to-day.
> One of my duties as such is to inspect the billets. They
> are scattered on all sides of the village, so quite an ap-
> preciable walk is entailed. The Orderly Sergeant and
> I had a drink of milk at one farm. We felt a little re-
> freshed after that. I mounted the guard with the Regi-
> mental Sergeant-Major. (Clements.) This afternoon he
> has been made Sergeant of the Transport, and has been
> succeeded as R.-S.-M. by Sergeant-Major Hoyle of B
> Company. Sergeant Preston becomes Company Ser-
> geant-Major of B Company.
>
> Yesterday the padre was appointed President of the
> Sports Committee, but, as the Colonel wanted to ar-
> range everything on his own lines—suggesting races in
> full pack, amongst other things!—he has resigned to-day.
>
> I had my first interview with Colonel Best-Dun-
> kley this morning. As Orderly Officer I was present
> at Commanding Officer's Orders. When he arrived at
> the Orderly Room he saw me and said:
>
> 'Who are you? Let me see, I don't think I have been
> introduced to you yet. How are you?'

I replied that my name was Floyd; and he shook hands quite genially!

There were only two cases up for orders. One man was there for cheeking a sergeant. He had called the sergeant something which cannot be repeated here.

'Why the b—— h—— did you speak to an N.C.O. like that?' exclaimed the Colonel in a Judge Jeffreys tone. 'Will you take my sentence? Or will you have a court martial?' he demanded.

The man replied that he would take the Colonel's sentence.

'Fourteen days Field Punishment No. 1,' snapped the Colonel. Exit prisoner.

After orders, Colonel Best-Dunkley asked me: 'What is your strong point?' I replied that I was sorry to have to say so, but I had none; I was not a specialist on anything. He did not even then become annoyed, but went on asking me one or two other questions. How long had I been gazetted? 'Not long,' was his comment on my reply. How long had I been in the Army? What unit was I in before? Where had I been educated? When I had answered these questions he expressed himself satisfied; so I saluted and departed. So I am on quite good terms with him so far, despite his terrible reputation! The question is—how long shall I remain on good terms with him? I wonder.

The next letter recounts one of those solemn Battalion parades which I recollect so well—those parades concerning which copious orders used to be issued the night before, and in preparation for which we were instructed in the formula which we (platoon commanders) had to employ when the Colonel, to the accompaniment of sweet sounds from the band, reached the edge of our platoons:

JUNE 14TH. We had a Battalion parade in a large field this morning. There was a long type-written programme of the ceremony to be gone through. We paraded on the company parade ground at 8 a.m. and the Colonel arrived on the Battalion parade ground at 9 a.m. He rode round the Battalion. When he reached my platoon he called me up to him and asked me whether I had a roll of my platoon. I replied that I had. He asked me whether I had it on me; and I replied that I had, and produced it. He seemed perfectly satisfied. He also asked me one or two other questions; to all of which I was able to give a satisfactory answer. And last night as I passed him in the road and saluted he smiled most affably and said 'good evening.' So he is quite agreeable with me so far. I do not therefore yet join in the general condemnation of him.

As far as I can tell at present his chief faults appear to me to be: that he suffers from a badly swelled head; that he fancies himself a budding Napoleon; that he is endowed by the fates with a very bad temper and a most vile tongue; that he is inconsiderate of his inferiors wherever his personal whims and ambitions are concerned; and that he is engrossed with an inordinate desire to be in the good graces of the Brigadier-General, who is really, I believe, a very good sort. Apart from those failings, some of which are, perhaps, excusable, I think he is probably all right.

You may be sure that his unpopularity will not prejudice me against him; I shall not join in the general condemnation unless and until he gives me good reason. As yet I have no such reason. Up to now his personality is merely a source of curiosity and amusement.

During the course of the morning's training, Captain Andrews rearranged the composition of the platoons in the Company; so I now command the eighth platoon. Sergeant Clews is the name of the platoon sergeant. Sergeant Dawson (who saw Norman Kemp killed and has the same high opinion of his heroic qualities as everybody else, whether officer, N. C. O., or man, who knew him; who tells me that he was by far the most loved officer in the Battalion—'one who will never be forgotten') is also in my platoon.

In the afternoon I went with the Company on a bathing parade. It was about half an hour's march. They bathed in a canal.

After tea I had a stroll in the country: it is very pretty, especially this weather....

Captain Andrews goes home on leave to-night; so Lieutenant Halstead is in command of B Company for a fortnight.

JUNE 15TH. The weather continues hot. We had another Battalion parade this morning: procedure the same as yesterday. The Colonel is still most agreeable; he has not said a cross word to me yet.

We took the afternoon easy, except that there was a parade for inspection of equipment at 4 p.m.

I received, this afternoon, a letter from you of June 11, and one from Mother of June 10, also enclosures. I am sorry to learn that you are both worrying. What's the use of worrying? What is there to worry about? I am quite safe. If I had the 'wind up' it might be another matter; but I do not, strange to say, even dread the time when we shall go back into the line! I think it rather exciting.

One is inclined to feel a little 'windy' when shells and 'minnies' are bursting dangerously near, or when a machine-gun spurts out of the gloaming; but there is a certain element of excitement about it all. I would not have missed those few days in the Salient for worlds. I had a pleasant 'baptism of fire' there. Everybody seems to think that it was worse than going over the top in a push. Those who fought at the Battle of the Somme last year say that they would rather be there than in the place where we were last week! Candidly, I cannot understand it.

We shall remain out of the line for some time yet— so cheer up!

CHAPTER 5

The March

I now come to one of the most remarkable, and in some re-
spects certainly the most comical, of all the episodes in which
Colonel Best-Dunkley figured—the memorable march from
Millain to Westbecourt. The following lengthy epistle which
I wrote in my billet in the Vale of Acquin at Westbecourt
the following day draws a perfectly accurate picture of what
happened:

JUNE 17TH. You will be interested to learn that we
have moved again. We are now billeted in a pretty little
village in the heart of north-eastern France....

Yesterday, Saturday June 16, 1917—the hundred
and second anniversary of Ligny and Quatre Bras—is
a day I am not likely ever to forget. Such a march we
had; and it was some stunt! Let me tell you, as far as I
can without naming places, the whole story.

Reveille sounded at 3 a.m. I rose at 5 a.m. We (the
officers) had breakfast at 5.30. Parade at 6. At 6.45 we
marched off from the village in which we had been billeted during the last few days. It was a very long march
which we had before us to the village in which we now
are—a distance of sixteen miles. Yet we were expecting
to arrive there by midday! I will show you how events
turned out so that we did not arrive here anything like
midday. The weather was, and is, just as it has been
all the time—a cloudless sky and a burning sun. It was

57

already quite warm when we set off, and as the morning advanced the sun naturally became more powerful still. We joined up with the rest of the Brigade a little further on, and marched past General Stockwell and Major Thompson (the Brigade-Major).

It was in the streets of Watten that we marched past Stockwell; and I vividly recollect that he was not at all pleased with things as early as that. I distinctly heard the word 'rabble' burst from his lips! The letter proceeds:

Men began to fall out before we reached the first village (or town as it happened to be). And as soon as the falling out began it continued without ceasing, only becoming more frequent the farther we got. I do think they began falling out too early. Every time a man fell out we subalterns had to drop behind with him and give him a chit. That naturally took time and one got right behind; then one would endeavour to catch up again; as soon as one was back with one's own platoon—generally before—one would come across more men of one's company who had fallen out, and so would get right back again. Thus it went on the whole time. It meant that we had double the walking to do that the men had; and we were loaded like Christmas trees just like them. Fortunately there was a mess cart with the Transport, containing still lemonade; so I had a drink now and then. It is an Army idea that one should not drink on the march: that it knocks one up much quicker. I say frankly, from experience, that it is nonsense. I drank as much as I could get hold of on the way (by no means as much as I could have drunk!) and though I was jolly tired I was as fresh as anybody else, and a good deal fresher than the majority, as you will see later. Well, after the first halt the falling out became dreadful; it was almost impossible for us to cope with the number of chits required; crowds must have been without chits at all. The whole roadside became one mass of exhausted men lying full length. Some were very bad indeed, some had sunstroke, some were sick, more than one were dying. At one time the padre and I were a long way behind, attending to these men. We hurried on to catch up the Battalion. The Transport, under Humfrey, were just behind the Battalion, so we followed along the Transport. When we got to the front end of it we saw nothing beyond! 'Where is the Battalion?' I asked Humfrey. He informed me that he had lost it. The Adjutant had, at the last turning, sent the Battalion one way and the Transport another; and he (Humfrey) had not the faintest idea where he was to go to! So he halted and got out a map. Then the Medical Officer (Adam) arrived on the scene too. We told him that the Battalion had disappeared. So we (Newman, Adam, Humfrey, and myself) sat down for about five minutes and discussed the situation. It struck us as being rather comical, though we wished that we were at the end of our journey instead of in a strange village and ignorant of which way we were to go. Humfrey decided to take his Transport the same way as the remainder of the Brigade Transport had gone; so we went on with him! We went across some very open country. The sun was simply burning down upon us. I felt very exhausted now; but I can stick almost anything in the way of a route march; no route march could, in my opinion, be as bad as that memorable Kidlington-Yarnton route march in March, 1916. The difficulty then was fatigue caused by the march through thick, soft slushy snow when vaccination was just at its worst; the difficulty this time was fatigue and thirst caused by the heat of a French summer. I admit that this route march yesterday was a stern test of endurance; but if I could stick the Kidlington-Yarnton stunt I could stick this, and I did stick this all the way, which very few others did! The trail which we left behind us was a sight to be seen: men, rifles, equipment, riderless horses all over; the Retreat from Moscow was spoken of! 'An utter fiasco, a debacle!' exclaimed Padre Newman.

Before we had gone with the Transport very far the Medical Officer was called round a corner to see a man who was reported to be dying; the padre went with him. I went on with the Transport. After a time I saw Lieutenant Reginald Andrews (the Adjutant) standing alone in a village; so it looked as if the remains of our Battalion must be somewhere about. A little further on I found Captain Blamey (O.C. D Company) and Giffin sitting by the side of the road. I asked them what they were doing, and they replied that they had fallen out with Sergeant-Major Howarth who was very bad indeed—reported to be dying. So the Battalion had passed that way.

I went on, and, in about ten minutes, saw ahead Colonel Best-Dunkley standing at the corner of a road branching off to the left from the road I was proceeding along with the Transport (just outside the village of Boisdinghem). Just as I reached this corner Brigadier-General Stockwell rode up from the opposite direction (on horseback) and, with a face wincing with wrath, accosted Colonel Best-Dunkley as follows:

'Dunkley, where's your Battalion?'

'This is my Battalion here, sir,' replied the Colonel, standing submissively to attention and indicating fifteen officers, non-commissioned officers, and men—all told—lying in a state of exhaustion at the side of this shaded country road.

'What! You call that a Battalion? Fifteen men! I call it a rabble. What the b—— h—— do you mean by it? Your Battalion is straggling all along the road right away back to (Watten)! You should have halted and collected them; not marched on like this. These men have not had a long enough halt or anything to eat all day. If this is the way you command a Battalion, you're not fit to command a Battalion. You're not even fit to command a platoon!'

The General then said that the Colonel, the Adjutant, and four company commanders could consider themselves 'under arrest'! The General was simply fuming with wrath; I do not think I have ever seen a man in such a temper. And I certainly never heard a colonel strafed in front of his own men before. It was an extraordinary scene. Those who have writhed under the venom of Colonel Best-Dunkley in the past would, doubtless, feel happy at this turning of the tables as it were, a refreshing revenge; but I must admit that my sympathy was with Colonel Best-Dunkley—and so was that of all present—in this instance, for we all felt that the General's censure was undeserved. It was not Colonel Best-Dunkley's fault; if it was anybody's fault it was the General's own fault for ordering the march by day instead of by night, and for not halting the Brigade for a long enough period earlier on in the course of the march. One felt that Colonel Best-Dunkley was being treated unjustly, especially as the North Lancs. had only arrived with ten! And the Irish had not yet arrived at all! (These facts must soon have become apparent to General Stockwell, and, perhaps, caused him, inwardly at any rate, to modify his judgment). And the way Colonel Best-Dunkley took it, the calm and submissive manner in which he bore General Stockwell's curses and the kind and polite way in which he afterwards gave orders to, and conversed with, his inferiors, both officers and men, endeared him to all. I consider that out of this incident Colonel Best-Dunkley has won a moral victory. He played his cards very well, and feeling changed towards him as a result.

The General went on: 'You yourself, the Adjutant,

and four mounted officers go right back to (Watten) immediately and collect your men together and bring them along here before you proceed any further.'

'I have sent two officers down the road, sir,' replied the Colonel.

'What the d——s the use of detailing unmounted officers for the job?' snapped General Stockwell. The Colonel said something else, and the General replied, 'That's no excuse.'

Then General Stockwell went off, and Colonel Best-Dunkley carried out his orders. We could see that we were now in for a very long halt here. It would take a deuce of a time to collect the Battalion together again! So we lay down under the shade of the roadside hedge and discussed the whole affair. Three sergeant-majors had fallen out on the way, two very bad indeed; officers had fallen out; and men wearing ribbons of the D.C.M. and the M.M., heroes of Gallipoli and the Somme, men who had never been beaten by a route march before, were lying along the country roads; so there must have been some reason for it! Amongst the sturdy fifteen were the new Regimental Sergeant-Major (Hoyle) and Sergeant-Major Preston of B Company; and there were also a few officers. The Transport made us some tea, which we enjoyed immensely. Humfrey had his little fox terrier, 'Darky,' who was born in the trenches at Thiepval during the Battle of the Somme last summer, with him. It is a nice little dog. I found a gold ring on the road just by me; and I intend to keep it as a souvenir of the episode.

We remained here for five hours—from 2.30 to 7.30. Men were reinforcing us all the time. After about half an hour General Stockwell appeared again. Glaring at Sergeant-Major Hoyle he addressed him as follows:

'Here are fifteen men whom I myself—I—have collected along the road. Get them some tea at once, sergeant-major!' He glanced at us all and then rode off again. He is clean-shaven and exceptionally young for a General; I should think he is not more than thirty-five. He is rather good-looking, but he has some temper. Some one remarked that General Stockwell and Colonel Best-Dunkley were men of similar temperament; on this occasion the latter had run up against the former; this interesting little episode at this country corner was the result!

There was an aerodrome near by (at Boisdinghem), and the Major there kindly sent his motor-lorries down the road to fetch up our men; so they kept arriving in motor-lorries the whole afternoon.

I can tell you we enjoyed this rest. One officer who had fallen out saw a mail motor-lorry. The driver said that he was looking for the (164) Brigade! So he got a lift. The mail arrived while we were resting in this shaded road; so I got your letter of June 12 and the enclosed letters, and read them there....

When we marched off again it was much cooler. The majority of the Battalion had been collected during the five hours, and we marched happily on—the band playing. The country was pretty, and everything was gay! The Colonel was awfully nice, inquiring whether the step was to our liking, and making himself agreeable in every possible way. All were pleased with him.

We arrived at our destination at 8.30, and the men were taken straight into the barns where they are billeted. Tea was served out immediately.

I am billeted in a farm again. The people are very decent indeed. The woman gave me three drinks as soon as I arrived, offering them herself and refusing to take any payment for them; she also offered to boil me a couple of eggs, but I did not wish to put on good nature any further. There is a nice little boy named

Edmond, aged fourteen. I talked to him in French as much as it was possible for me to do in that language. He cannot speak English....

Allen and I are both billeted in the same room here. B Company Mess is in a house close by, and B Company are billeted in the barns of a farm almost opposite.

The village we are in (Westbecourt) is geographically divided into two parts, north and south. The southern portion, in which we are, is a valley (le Val d'Acquin). The northern part is on the reverse slope of a hill which lies on the other side of the valley. Battalion Headquarters is at a farm on that northern side of the high ground, just by the church.

We rose at 10 a.m. this morning. The weather today has been hotter than ever. One perspires even when quite still. The sun has been scorching down. We had an inspection at 11, and the M. O. came round to inspect the men's feet at 2.40. Just as he was going away the Colonel turned up at the farm where B Company is in billets. He was on horseback, in slacks and in his shirt-sleeves; to live in one's shirt sleeves is a very common custom this weather. He informed us that General Stockwell is coming to inspect the Battalion to-morrow!

During the day I have been exploring the village. It is very pretty indeed, much prettier than the last place we were at. There are thick woods, green fields, shaded avenues—some completely arched by all kinds of trees; and, the district being hilly, the country is thus all the more charming. Milk is very cheap here. I got a big bowl of milk for 1d. at one farm in the valley the other side of the hill. It is splendid here; and we are likely to remain here some time.

At 7.40 the padre conducted a short voluntary church parade service in an orchard behind the farm in which C Company hangs out—just opposite the farm in which I am billeted. Allen, Priestley, Barker, Giffin, and I were there. The band was there for the first hymn—it then had to go to Headquarters to play 'retreat' at 8 p.m. There were about twenty men....

Sergeant-Major Howarth, D. C. M., died at St. Omer that day, overpowered by the march of the previous day. "He was not at all the class of man one can afford to lose, and his loss was greatly deplored," comments the Lancashire Fusiliers' Annual. And Sergeant-Major Howarth was not, I believe, the only casualty of the kind caused by the march.

Before I close this chapter I ought to say a word about the Brigadier whose personality dominates the canvas. I do not wish it to be supposed that I desire to reflect in any way upon the character and ability of General Stockwell. Nothing could be further from my mind. I relate the incident because it strikes me as being funny, because such an episode forms the subject for an interesting study in the bearing of two remarkable personalities, and because I hold that the truth should always be told about such matters. The episode has long been a topic of intimate conversation amongst members of the 2/5th Lancashire Fusiliers and their friends; many a laugh have we had about it. Why should not the public be allowed to laugh with us?

All men and women, even the greatest, are capable of making mistakes. Nobody is perfect. Even the great Napoleon made mistakes. So General Stockwell will not, I am sure, claim to be immaculate. But for Clifton Inglis Stockwell as a General I entertain, and always have entertained, feelings of the most profound respect. Nobody can possibly entertain a more ardent devotion for a leader than I entertain for General Stockwell under whom it has been my good fortune to have the honour to serve in 1917, in 1918, and in 1919. The longer I have served under him the more have I admired his perfectly obvious talent, his brilliant initiative, and his striking personality. His record in the Great War is unique.

As a captain in the Royal Welsh Fusiliers, he commanded a company in the retreat from Mons in 1914. He rose rapidly. He became a major; and he became a colonel; and, during the Battle of the Somme, in 1916, he became a Brigadier-General, succeeding Brigadier-General Edwards in command of the 164th Brigade. And he remained in command of that famous Brigade until the end of the war. As I studied the countenance of General Stockwell on that country road at Boisdinghem that afternoon I realized that he was no ordinary twopenny-halfpenny brigadier; but I did not then know that this was the man who, less than twelve months later, was destined to stand between Ludendorff and decisive victory in his last dramatic throw at Givenchy on the glorious ninth of April, and seven months later still to be chosen to command the flying column known by his name which captured Ath on Armistice Day and fired the last shots of the Great War. It is right that Stockwell's place in history should be duly appreciated.

CHAPTER 6

The General's Speech

This chapter will be a very short one; but, despite its brevity, it seems to me that the event narrated in it should form the subject of a single chapter. General Stockwell's speech at Westbecourt, on Waterloo day, 1917, was a very remarkable speech; it was the most striking speech I have ever heard—and I have listened to a good many famous public speakers in my time—and it produced a very profound impression upon all who heard it. I only wish there had been a reporter present to take it down verbatim. But that could not be. Those were the days of that most objectionable of all tyrants, the Censor! I can but quote from the letter which I wrote home from Westbecourt:

JUNE 18TH. The Battalion paraded in a field just by my billet this morning. General Stockwell arrived at 10.45. The General Salute, Present Arms, was ordered by Best-Dunkley. The General rode up, and, facing the Battalion, said to Best-Dunkley: 'All right; slope arms, order arms, stand at ease, and close up your companies.' The Colonel gave the required orders. General Stockwell then addressed the Battalion. 'Colonel Best-Dunkley, gentlemen, non-commissioned officers, and men of the 2/5th Lancashire Fusiliers, I am very sorry indeed to have to say what I am going to say to you now'—he began. He then spoke about the march of Saturday, drew a vivid picture of the scene as it appeared to him, said that he had had very great faith in the discipline of this Battalion and was very sorry that under stress our discipline should prove so weak; said that the Brigade had been selected for the most difficult and trying part in the forthcoming operations (he then told us what part: I cannot, of course, reveal what!) because Sir Douglas Haig considers us the best brigade in the Division, and that if we could not stick Saturday what would we do then? He remarked that the Lancashire Fusiliers had won more V. C.'s than any other regiment in the British Army, and he closed by saying that he would still trust us, and hoped that we would act up to our traditions in the future.

Having said his say he disappeared as quickly as he had appeared!

We then carried on with training. We finished at 12. The weather is still hot.

I had a stroll about the village this afternoon, having some milk again at the farm I spoke of yesterday.

At 6.15 this evening we were all summoned to a conference at Battalion Headquarters. Colonel Best-Dunkley told us all about a new scheme of training which commences to-morrow and also explained to us the plan of campaign and what part we are to play, with reference to the exact points on the map, in the next great battle, which he said would be the greatest battle of the war. It is a thing which I have always thought ought to be done. And I may say that I am of a very decided opinion that if it is a complete success there is not a shade of doubt but that peace will be signed in September; but unless it is a complete success we shall have to wait for Maude and Murray in Asia Minor.... This battle is not going to be fought just yet; we have to practise it all first!

There is no harm in telling you that the Colonel told us that we should remain billeted in this village for the remainder of this month at least. And it is a delightful little village to be in. But we are an hour and a half's march from the divisional training area where we are now going to proceed for training every day....

Every time June 18 comes round I cannot help thinking of the great drama brought to a close on that day in 1815. Before many weeks have passed I myself will probably partake in the operations of another Waterloo fought upon the blood-stained soil of unhappy Belgium! I always said that I would be in at the finish whether that finish happens to be in Belgium, on the Rhine, or in Palestine, didn't I?

Yes, It was my destiny to be "in at the finish;" but the finish was not, as so many of our optimists then thought it would be, at Ypres in 1917! The decisive victory was not to be ours until Foch and Sir Henry Wilson were at the head of military affairs and D'Esperey at Cerna and Allenby at Armageddon had won their Waterloo in the September of 1918; and when Stockwell's Force fired the last shots at Ath in Belgium I was there!

CHAPTER 7

The Vale of Acquin

We now commenced that early rising and continuous
training with which we soon became heartily "fed up."

JUNE 19TH. I rose at 3.30 this morning, made a hurried breakfast, and went on parade at 4.15. We marched
about three miles to the training area. Our dress on this
occasion was without tunics, but Sam Brown and other
articles of equipment over our shirts; shirt-sleeves rolled
up. When we reached very open country, high up on
the moorland, a thunder-storm came on and we were
drenched! It was splendid. As we were wet through, we
marched back to our village again when it got fine! It
was quite fine again when we got back. It is just a little
cooler now, but is quite fine and warm.

At 11 we had a conference at Battalion Headquarters. The Colonel informed us that we are moving again,
after all, to-morrow! We are going to another village
eighteen miles away. I expect the reason is because the
selected training area for us while here is not satisfactory. I am sorry we are moving again so soon, because I
like this village....

JUNE 20TH. ....An order came round yesterday evening
to the effect that we might move to the new place by
bus, it might be by march; in case it should be the latter
we must be prepared to move off at 2 in the morning. Later in the evening Regimental Sergeant-Major

Hoyle came to see us in B Company Officers' Mess, as he frequently does by invitation, and told us that it was now official that we were to move by motor-bus at 7 this morning; so we all decided to go to bed.

We got up at 4.30 this morning and had breakfast. We were then informed that the move was 'washed out' for to-day, and that we were to carry on with training. A parade was ordered, and took place at 6.30, for the purpose of proceeding to the training area as per yesterday; but it rained, and the parade was dismissed with orders to stand by until further orders. Then a box-respirator inspection in billets, with drill on same, was ordered and took place; it was, I may incidentally remark, the second they had already had during the day.

This kind of thing went on for some time; the weather cleared up; and then another parade was ordered and took place at 9.15. We then marched off to the training area. We went four or five miles this time, further than we went yesterday. We passed through that village where the padre and I lost the Battalion on the march here on Saturday! We halted in a field beyond that village. Then Colonel Best-Dunkley asked for all officers. We all sat round him on the grass for about a quarter of an hour while he explained to us a tactical scheme which the Battalion was now to carry out in the district.

We then carried out the tactical scheme which took place over potato fields and fine crops—it seemed a great pity for the farmers! We all had to move our platoons across country to a certain position, each platoon proceeding separately, but, of course, keeping its correct distance from the others, and, by means of scouts and runners, keeping in communication.

On the front along which I had to proceed with my platoon there were numerous fields enclosed by thick hedges and awkward obstacles; but I got it along all right, without either map or compass. In one lane I

71

encountered Major Brighten, sitting on horseback. He asked me various questions about the position, and gave me a word or two of advice. I really like Major Brighten very much; he is the nicest, as well as one of the most capable, officer in the Battalion. When the scheme was over, Halstead told me that my platoon was in exactly the right position. That information was a pleasant surprise!

We then marched back. Some of the way I rode on Halstead's horse, 'Peter.' He must be a very good horse, because I got along all right; he did not play any pranks. We got back at 3.45.... We had a kind of lunch at 4 p.m. At 5.30 we attended a conference of all officers at Battalion Headquarters. The Colonel discussed the scheme, and criticized most officers very roundly; fortunately he had nothing whatever to say about me! While we were there the Adjutant opened an order from Brigade to the effect that the move is now cancelled altogether; so we are remaining here for our training. I am glad.

JUNE 21ST. We were up at 4 again this morning. I am becoming very 'fed up' with this stupidly early rising. I have no particular objection to shells or to route marches in themselves; but I do object to being awakened from a pleasant sleep and having to get up at 4 every morning! It makes one feel so washed out.

At 5 we marched off on a Battalion route march. We went round about nine miles, and got back at 9.45. Then there was a kit inspection; then gas drill. This afternoon I had a stroll in the woods. There was a foot inspection at 4; there is a battle-order inspection at 5.40; and this evening there is to be bayonet fighting and bombing! The men are, quite naturally, not pleased.

JUNE 22ND. We marched off at 6 this morning to a range about seven miles away (at Cormette). When we had been going about twenty minutes it began to rain.

It rained all the way, but we went on just the same. I had no coat, so was thoroughly wet. When we got to the range it was still raining. We had lunch there and discussed whether to fire or not. We got there at 9. At 11 it was decided to return without firing.

This, I remember, was the occasion upon which I first met John Bodington, who had just returned to the Battalion, from leave I suppose. He was then second-in-command of D Company, and did not possess a single ribbon. Few could have guessed what a remarkable military future lay before him. "I should guess he's about the luckiest fellow that ever dodged a 5.9," remarked a friend, now on the Rhine, who wrote to me the other day (August 11, 1919).

It simply poured on the way back. I was drenched to the skin. I do not think I have ever had such a drenching before. The ground was thick with mud and slush. We were all horribly dirty. It was 2 p.m. when we got back. I took off my things and had them dried by the fire. The people in this billet are really very decent indeed. I went to bed for an hour. Then tea. At 6 we had a lecture on the compass, by Major Brighten.

JUNE 23RD. Reveille was not quite so early as usual this morning. We did not march off from here until 8 a.m. We then went, in battle-order, to the training area. While there I saw, through my field-glasses, General Sir Hubert Gough, Lieutenant-General Sir Herbert Watts, Major-General Jeudwine, and Brigadier-General Stockwell, on horseback, together with a whole crowd of staff-officers, on the crest of a hill some distance away. They were too far off for their faces to be distinguishable; but I knew that they were the above-mentioned generals because Major Brighten told us yesterday that they were coming. They were inspecting the training.

The weather to-day has been very nice—sunshine, yet neither too hot nor too cold. We got back at 2. Then lunch. I then went to the farm the other side of the hill for some milk. Then tea. Then bombing. Then dinner. Then letter-writing. Now bed!

Would you mind sending me a Lancashire Fusilier cap badge? Excuse me asking for something fresh in every letter, but Colonel Best-Dunkley has conceived the brilliant idea that our battalion should set an example to the rest of the Brigade—'lead the way,' as he calls it—by having cap badges in our steel helmets as well as in our soft hats. Of course with such devices we cannot fail to defeat the enemy next time we encounter him! What a life!

We are hoping, but scarcely daring to expect, that a somewhat easier day will be ours to-morrow, Sunday!

JUNE 24TH. I did not get up until 9 this morning. Church parade was at 10. The service was, of course, taken by Newman.... The service was held in the field which is the Battalion parade ground. After the service the padre had a communion service in a corner of the field for those who wished to stay. About twenty men stayed, and the following officers—Colonel Best-Dunkley, Allen, Gratton, Giffin and myself. The padre had a miniature oak altar, containing a crucifix, with two lighted candles, on a table.

After this Colonel Best-Dunkley walked down the lane with us and accepted Giffin's invitation to come inside B Company's Mess. He had a drink with us there, and stayed a minute or two. He remarked that it was a dirty mess, pointed out a match on the floor, and, with his customary blink and twitch of the nose, asked how we dare ask him into such a dirty mess; but he also paid us the compliment of saying that B Company was the best working company in the Battalion! Then we walked up to Headquarters with him as he wanted us there. He told us that Sir Hubert Gough expressed himself pleased with the Battalion yesterday. When we got to Headquarters he gave us a paper to answer—an account of an operation upon which we were each to write a report. We then returned and wrote out the reports. Then lunch.

The weather has been glorious to-day—bright sunshine, with a refreshing breeze, not too hot. This afternoon I had a walk in the country beyond this village, and strolled about a thickly-clustered wood, plucking wild strawberries and eating them. Then back for tea. Then letter censoring.

We are supposed to do an hour's reading per day of military text-books, and have to send in to Orderly Room a certificate to that effect every evening!

JUNE 25TH. We have been to the range again to-day. A and B Companies went later than the others, so we did not leave here until 8.45. It was 11.45 when we got there. The weather was glorious as usual; and, since there was a slight breeze, it was not too hot. We got the men into details of eight and fired this time. We had taken our lunch with us, and so we had it there. The ground there (at Cormette) is very high, and there is a splendid view. I put my glass on it. We remained there until 4. Then we marched back....

I had three sergeants with my platoon to-day—Sergeant Clews, the platoon-sergeant, Sergeant Dawson, and Sergeant Baldwin. The latter I like very much; he is a very pleasant youth; he was a corporal in 7th Platoon when I first joined the Battalion. My four section commanders in 8th Platoon are Corporal Pendleton (Bombers), Lance-Corporal Morgan (Rifleman), Lance-Corporal Flint (Rifle Grenadiers, and Gas N. C. O.), and Lance-Corporal Riley (Lewis Gunners). Lance-Corporal Topping, of 7th Platoon, lives in Oldham Road, Middleton; he is a nice easy-going boy; I like him very much. He told me, when we were out on that working party on June 9, that he knew my face.

Since I am on this subject I might mention that there are the following sergeants in B Company: Sergeant-Major Preston, Quartermaster-Sergeant Jack, Sergeant Donovan, Sergeant Butterworth, Sergeant Williams, and the three I have mentioned above. I think the most competent N. C. O. in my platoon, apart from Dawson, who does not command a section, and Baldwin, who really belongs to 7th Platoon, is Corporal Pendleton. My servant is Critchley. He is, of course, in my platoon. He is a very obliging man. I am perfectly satisfied with him. Officers' servants also act as runners. I think it is a bit thick on the part of the Colonel making them go on parade; it means that they have very little time to themselves.

The B Company officers are: Captain Andrews (Officer Commanding), Lieutenant Halstead (Second-in-Command) who is Company Commander while Captain Andrews is on leave, Lieutenant Giffin (a Rossall boy who, with the traditional Rossall touch, tries to play the 'senior sub' part—always ticking one off and making personal remarks), Second-Lieutenant Allen, Second-Lieutenant Gratton, and myself. Gratton was a private in Gallipoli, and so is a decent sort. Allen is very orthodox and proper, and gets very 'windy' about being on parade in time; but he is a good sort and we are great friends. He comes from Buxton way somewhere. Gratton comes from the south; he was in the Royal Fusiliers as a Tommy. Halstead comes from Haslingden; he is a very decent, calm, fellow. He is married. Giffin comes from Burnley. He is about my age. Gratton is twenty-seven. The two latter were on leave when I arrived.

Two new officers have recently arrived from Scarborough—Walsh and Hickey. They arrived there from cadet battalions just before I came out here. They are in

A Company, which is at present commanded by Captain Briggs, Captain Cochrane being on leave. Lieutenant Ronald, an Argyll and Sutherland Highlander attached to this Battalion—a decent sort—is also in A Company; he has just been on leave. Leave comes round in turn throughout the officers of the Battalion; it will be a long time before my turn comes: perhaps when the war is over! Horace Beesley of D Company is very nice with me; he is an awfully decent sort. Lieutenant Joye, who is in command of Headquarters Company, is an amusing fellow; he is large and fat, with yellow hair and a smiling face. Colonel Best-Dunkley is always going for him; he had him under open arrest for something paltry the other day! Lieutenant West is Assistant Adjutant and also physical training officer. Captain Bodington is in command of D Company while Captain Blamey is on leave. Reggie Andrews, the Adjutant, amuses me. He does not seem to worry much, though the Colonel gives him a deuce of a time; he is very short-sighted, but does not wear glasses. He is very young.

I am Orderly Officer to-day and have not performed a single duty appertaining thereto! It was too late to mount the guard when I got back from the range; and the Colonel had a conference of all officers this evening at the time when staff parade was being held. These conferences are a bore. The Colonel blinks and twitches his nose, and the thing dawdles on. The subject of the conference on this occasion was to discuss a Brigade scheme taking place on the training area on Wednesday.

JUNE 27TH. We have had hardly a moment to ourselves during the last two days. At 9 yesterday morning we walked to the training area, as all officers and N. C. O.'s had to reconnoitre the area in which the Brigade stunt was to take place to-day. When we got a little

77

beyond the aerodrome, Allen, Verity, Barker and I got a lift in a Flying Corps tender as far as (Cormette), the little village where we had to assemble at 10. We then went over the area using maps, and the scheme was explained. The area was exactly the same in dimensions as that with which we shall have to deal in the great battle, and positions were named by the names of positions which we shall attack then; strong points were marked by rings of flags. We spent a terribly long time up there; we sat down waiting for company commanders to return for about two hours. The whole thing, I am sure, could have been done in much less time. The position of advance allotted to our Battalion was on the extreme left of the Brigade, B Company on the left of the Battalion, and 8th Platoon, therefore, on the extreme left of the Brigade....

It was nearly 5 p.m. before we got back, having had no lunch. We had some then. At 6.30 we had to attend a conference at Battalion Headquarters. It was 8 when we got back to B Company Mess, so then dinner; and at 9.15 we were on parade for marching off on this Brigade stunt! It was midnight when the Battalion reached the village where we had assembled in the morning; we felt very tired and sleepy. The first thing we did was to get all the dispositions of the Battalion (the same happened throughout the whole Brigade) effected under darkness, every section in its correct place. The dew had fallen very thickly and the long grass and corn were wringing wet; consequently we all got our feet and legs soaked. Then dummy ammunition was distributed. At about 2 a.m. we had permission to lie down where we were and get some sleep if we could! I lay down in the dirt at the roadside and had an hour or two's sleep. At about 3.30, when it was becoming light, I was awakened, my teeth chattering horribly, hearing the Brigadier-General strafing somebody! General Stockwell and his Staff seemed to be walking up and down all night. I saw them just before I went to sleep, and the first object which I saw on opening my eyes again was General Stockwell. I hear that poor Best-Dunkley got it hot again from the Brigadier about something during the night! The fiery young General seemed to be on the war-path.

At 5.15 we had breakfast, cooked in the travelling cook-wagons. We had to keep going up and down the line most of the time, explaining the scheme to the section commanders. Then Colonel Best-Dunkley went along the line asking questions. The first section commander he dropped on was poor Topping, who had only been put on the particular job last night; he had been somewhere else yesterday when it was all explained. The Colonel asked him what was the interval between his section and the section on his right; he did not know! 'You see, your section commanders don't know their orders,' blinked the Colonel.

7th and 8th platoons were merged into one under Giffin. I commanded the left wing, consisting of the sections of Lance-Corporal Topping and Lance-Corporal Heap. We were the fourth wave, supporting the two platoons of Gratton and Allen who were in the third wave. The idea was that another brigade had taken all the strong points, and our brigade had to push forward past them and penetrate the enemy's lines to a certain distance, consolidate, and repel counter-attacks. The other brigades were supposed to have gone over the top at dawn. So we went over at 7 a.m. We went forward very nicely, under cover of a 'creeping barrage' which was represented by drums rumbling and flags waving. At the little village of (Noir Carme) Giffin went to the right, and I took Topping's and Heap's sections through the village and round to a field the other side where I turned half-left and awaited Giffin's arrival on the right.

When he came up we all advanced to our final objective which was in advance of the Battalion's objective. We have to go to the outpost line. Then we sent off flares to signal to the aircraft that we had reached our objective; and then we were supposed to be digging in and putting out wire, patrolling, and resisting counterattacks! As a matter of fact we sat there for a an hour or two. My two sections were on the extreme left of the whole Brigade.

At 11.30 the stunt was declared over and the men went home; but General Stockwell wished to see all the officers in the Brigade. So we assembled near the aerodrome. The General was very agreeable; he was in a most agreeable and accommodating mood; he seemed very pleased indeed with everything. He spoke for about twenty minutes on the operations. He is really a brilliant speaker. He said that on the whole the advance was carried out very well indeed, that the right was not quite so good, but that the left was very good indeed; we kept our dressing splendidly! Giffin and I exchanged glances of satisfaction.

At the close of his speech General Stockwell said that we must do the scheme once or twice again, and asked the colonels (Best-Dunkley, Hindle, Heath, and Balfour) whether 9.30 to-morrow morning would be agreeable on the training area. Colonel Best-Dunkley said that it would do quite well; but Colonel Heath objected that the men were all tired and would require some sleep— would not Friday be better? 'Very well then; I'm quite agreeable to have it on Friday; you can do what you like to-morrow,' replied the General in a jovial tone. We were all very pleased. The conference over we set off back. Thus ended our first 'dress rehearsal'!

When we got back we had some lunch. Then, at 2 in the afternoon we went to bed. At 5.30 Critchley wakened me with the information that there was a conference of all officers at the aerodrome at 6. Allen immediately got the 'wind up,' but I pointed out to him that even if it were correct, which I doubted, the thing was now out of the question so far as we were concerned; so we might as well remain in bed and get up at our leisure. As a matter of fact, the information turned out to be incorrect: it was merely company commanders who were required—Halstead had gone.

We got up for dinner at 8. Captain Andrews had then returned from leave. When Halstead got back he was jolly glad to find that he was relieved from the responsibilities and worries of a company commander. But Captain Andrews is going to be second-in-command of the Battalion in the forthcoming battle, as Major Brighten, who is now home on leave, may not be there; so Halstead will have to command B Company in the operations, and this scheme is to hold good, with regard to all schemes and rehearsals concerning the operations.

JUNE 29TH. We are working very hard just now, and it is all I can do to find time to write letters; one's natural inclination is to sleep when one has an afternoon free after a strenuous morning, but some letters must be written, so I must write.

Yesterday morning we rose at 8.30 and had breakfast. Then we received notification that all officers and N. C. O.'s were to parade at the aerodrome at 10.30 for a lecture. So we walked there. There was not much of a lecture. A Royal Flying Corps officer explained some aeroplane signals to us, and then an aeroplane went up and exhibited them. Then we were told that we could dismiss. So we walked back again. We all thought it a 'wash out' having us up there just for that. Colonel Best-Dunkley stayed behind to have a fly. I will not repeat the hopes which were expressed by certain of his battalion! He flew over our village and dropped a message at Battalion Headquarters. All went off without any accidents!

We had lunch when we got back. Then I censored two hundred letters. We had a thunder-storm and a heavy fall of rain in the evening. I went to bed soon after dinner. There was no mail yesterday.

This morning we rose at 5.30. We marched off at 6.30 and did the Brigade stunt again on the training area. I am getting rather fed up with Giffin on parade. He nearly landed me in the soup this morning by his dictatorial interference; he seems to like to make one realize that he is a full lieutenant! When I had got Topping's section down on to the road just before the village he signalled for me to bring it back again. The result was a 'box-up,' and we got right behind our wave, whereas if we had gone straight on we would have kept in line; but, fortunately, I got right again in a few minutes. We finished at 12.40. Then all officers had to attend a conference with the General again. General Stockwell was very pleased with the show, and had no complaints. I am getting to like General Stockwell very much; his face is not unlike that of the great Sir David Beatty.

We felt jolly tired after it all. It was hot and tiring walking back. We got back at 3 p.m. Then lunch. Giffin had the decency to apologize for his nastiness. 'I hope you did not mind me cursing you this morning, Floyd,' he said. I replied that I did not, but said that I thought that it would have been better for me to go on when I had got on the road. Of course, he did not agree! When on the march if I call out a step he washes it out and says that it is the wrong one. And he is always criticizing one. Halstead is very different; he does not interfere with one; in fact, he has complimented me on all occasions of these schemes. After the General had mentioned that the left did so well the other day Halstead said in the

Mess: 'Yes, our left flank was fine, thanks to Floyd; he managed it like a general.' That is, of course exaggeration in the opposite direction; I make no claim to any talents of that kind: but it is encouraging for one's company commander to talk like that, more encouraging than the way the second-in-command, Giffin, behaves. Giffin is quite agreeable generally, but I do not like his patronizing air.

We have packed and sent off our kit-bags this evening, as we are returning to the trenches in a day or two. So if you do not get any letters for a few days shortly, do not get the wind up; I will write whenever I have time....

I am rather surprised to hear of the change in the Mediterranean Command. I gather that Sir Archibald Murray, towards whom I entertained such complete confidence, is sharing the fate of his famous predecessor, Sir Ian Hamilton; for I learn that Sir Edmund Allenby, the victor of Arras, is leaving France to take command in Egypt. Sir Julian Byng has been appointed to command the Third Army in his place, and General Byng is succeeded by General Currie as commander of the Canadian Corps. Things have certainly been very quiet in Palestine lately; but I think that is the fault of Sir William Robertson in taking Douglas' 42nd Division away from Murray; but poor Murray gets sacked because he fails to get on when supplied with insufficient troops! I am sorry. I had pictured Sir Archibald Murray leading a victorious wing at Armageddon, but that, apparently, is not now to be: Sir Edmund Allenby reigns in his stead. Perhaps the new general will have more troops sent out to him; perhaps we shall now get a move on in Palestine, so important a theatre of operations; the arrival of Sir Edmund Allenby in the East may prove the signal for a fresh offensive out there. Sir Stanley Maude has been very quiet lately; but I suppose the weather will be adverse to operations in Mesopotamia at present. I wonder why something is not done with Sir George Milne's force at Salonica. Apparently all is not even yet plain sailing in Greece. There is still intrigue going on. I do not think Venizelos is going to have everything his own way, even now King Constantine has gone to Switzerland. Switzerland is now, I think, the theatre of important diplomatic intrigues. I think King Constantine's abdication is only temporary; I think King Alexander only reigns for the period of the war. Do not fret—King Constantine knows what he is doing!

What about Holland? There seems to be trouble there. And, as Father remarks, Ireland is troublesome again; but Sir Bryan Mahon ought to be able to deal with the insurgents, even though Lord Wimborne is still Viceroy; and Duke is a better Chief Secretary than Birrell!

How is Lord Rhondda going on as Food Controller? Are things any better than they were under Devonport? Lloyd George seems to be declining in popularity. And the people seem determined not to have Churchill in office! So what will happen? Things are very quaint at present.

Well, darkness has descended upon the country-side; it is time I was retiring to rest; I therefore lay down my pen. Good night!

My diary, under date June 30, states:

"A quiet morning. Inspections. Then went to see relief plan of area of our forthcoming attack in a field at Boisdinghem."

Thus ended our long rest. The evening of June 30—our last at Westbecourt—is one which is still well remembered by those who were there, and still much spoken of by those who were not there! It was a lively evening in the various company messes. Champagne was much in demand, and "all went merry as a marriage bell." I will never forget the fun we had in B Company Mess that evening. I laughed for two hours without ceasing. At 11 p.m. I returned to my billet whence the staid and quiet Allen had already preceded me. I talked volubly to him for about a quarter of an hour, apparently causing him considerable amusement, and then would insist on going back to the mess for my Church Times which I had left there. When I got there the mess was locked up, so I had to return without it! The most amusing point about this episode is that an officer who was in another company mess at the time has always professed to know more about the happenings in B Company Mess that evening than any B Company officers who were present

CHAPTER 8

Back to the Salient

We returned to Ypres on July 1. Everybody was thinking and talking about the great Battle on the Somme of which this was the first anniversary; but before the day was over we ourselves had cause to remember the first of July.

My diary contains a brief synopsis of the journey:

JULY 1ST. Up 4 a.m. Breakfast 4.40. Marched off from Westbecourt at 6.15. Marched to Lumbres. The place full of Portuguese. Entrained there. Train left Lumbres at 10 a.m. Went through St. Omer, Hazebrouck, and Poperinghe. We got out at Brandhoek, about two miles beyond Poperinghe—nearly at Vlamertinghe. Marched to Query Camp. Remained here in tents during the afternoon. The arrangements concerning us seem very vague. Divisional Staff do not appear to have given very definite orders to General Stockwell. But one thing is known: we are to relieve the 165th Brigade in the trenches in the Ypres Salient. At Query Camp we are about three miles from the German front line, and so well within range of the guns. They are booming as usual all the time.

In a letter written home from the Ramparts the following day, I described our return to the Salient as follows:

JULY 2ND. Yesterday, Sunday, was our last day in reserve billets. We rose at 4 a.m. At 6.15 we marched off. We marched to a village about an hour and a half's march away—a village where there are some Portuguese troops. There we entrained. We left at about 10 a.m. We travelled to the railhead where I got off on my arrival on June 5; but this time the train took us about two miles beyond the station. Then we marched to a camp about three miles behind the front line. We remained there, in tents, all the afternoon. Colonel Best-Dunkley came into B Company's mess tent. He was so taken up with the arrangements which Allen, the mess president, had made that he remained for tea with us! He was in a very agreeable mood; he is certainly a man of moods. He tried to put the wind up me about life in the trenches, but did not succeed. The Adjutant was there too, also Captain Andrews and an officer from the brigade we are relieving. Nobody else seemed disposed to come in. The Colonel dined at Division, which was the other side of some trees; but the Adjutant remained for dinner with us. Gratton asked me to show my Middleton Guardian correspondence to the Adjutant, and I did so; he was very interested. West, the Assistant Adjutant, also read it.

While we were at Query Camp orders came round to all companies that one officer per company was to be detailed to leave at 5 p.m. and proceed to the Salient and reconnoitre the trenches. Captain Andrews detailed Halstead to go from B Company. Ronald went from A, Barker from C, and Wood from D. They all set off together. Giffin also left us, as he was detailed to take over billets for us in the Prison.

At 8.40 we moved off. We went at intervals of three hundred yards between platoons, with six connecting files. As Giffin had been sent on much earlier to 'take over,' I was in command of the combined 7th and 8th platoons. I had four sergeants with me—Sergeant Williams and Sergeant Clews in front, and Sergeant Dawson and Sergeant Baldwin behind. At first I marched in front, but then Captain Andrews told me to march in rear of my platoon; so I chatted with Sergeant Baldwin for the rest of the way. He is twenty years old and has been in the Army since he was seventeen. He joined the Argyles in 1914, and was stationed in Edinburgh for some time. Then he was discharged on account of weak eyesight. But he immediately enlisted again; this time in the Lancashire Fusiliers. His home is Higher Broughton. His father, who is forty-nine, is a sergeant in the Manchesters at Salonica; I believe he said that he was wounded.

Things were moderately quiet until we reached the (Prison). It was about 10 p.m. when we got there. Things then became much livelier; shells were bursting all round. We found the building uninhabitable. The casualties there during the last few days have been very heavy. One shell buried a party in the debris; it took four hours' solid digging to get them out! So it has been decided to abandon the place as a billet.

We were delayed here because we thought this was our destination; but we were informed that we were to go on to some ramparts, wherever they might be! I had not the faintest idea where they were. Anyhow I followed those in front along the ghastly streets of the city. Shells were dropping all round. One shell exploded ten yards away. A moment later Sergeant Baldwin and I noticed one of the men in rear of the platoon fainting and pulling horrible faces. I asked him whether he was hit. It appeared that he had got shell-shock. So we got hold of him and called out for the stretcher-bearers. Meanwhile, we got completely out of the platoon; they, of course, went on. So we were left behind by ourselves. A stretcher-bearer turned up in a minute or two; then another. So we got Private Armstead off to the nearest dug-out we could find; it happened to be a Brigade Headquarters of some other brigade. There was a Medical Officer there; so he saw to the man, and gave me a chit to take back with me concerning him. Baldwin and I thought that we might as well have a rest for a short time as it was quite comfortable here! So we did. I happened to have a couple of oranges in my haversack, so we each had one; we then felt refreshed. At about 11.40 we thought it would not be a bad idea to get a move on; so we went outside amongst the nasty shells again. It was decidedly exciting in that we did not know how far we had to go, or whether we were ever likely to find the dug-outs whither our platoon had gone! We kept asking everybody we passed whether they had 'seen any L. F.'s?' We thus kept in the right direction as we were generally told that they had gone over yonder! We came to a spot having a very sinister tradition attached to it (the Menin Gate). So we doubled across here as fast as possible! Eventually we managed to find the dug-outs where our people were. We had arrived safe and sound. So Baldwin went to his dug-out with the others and I looked for Captain Andrews and reported to him when I found him. I then went into my dug-out, which is the same one as his. It is very cosy. I lit a candle and read the four letters which I had received by the mail which arrived just before we left the tents, and also the newspapers which you have sent....

As regards the papers—they are very interesting indeed. The Mesopotamian Commission Report seems to have caused a great sensation. A good many public men are censured. I am glad to find that the one reputation made, or rather restored, is that of Earl Curzon! I have been discussing it with Captain Andrews at breakfast this morning. We had breakfast in the mess dug-out at 12 this morning. The other B Company officers stayed in bed for breakfast.

There was an inspection of box-respirators and rifles this afternoon. I inspected my own platoon, which is now 7 again! with Sergeant Baldwin. I happened to re-mark to him that I presumed that he was now platoon sergeant of this platoon. He said that he was. 'That's all right,' I replied; and he smiled. Then Giffin, who must have overhead our remarks, approached and, in his im-perious way, said: 'Sergeant Baldwin, you're only in charge of 7 Platoon temporarily, until Sergeant But-terworth comes back; you're not platoon sergeant. You understand that, Floyd?' he concluded, turning to me. I think it a bit thick that one cannot choose one's own platoon sergeant....

Halstead has not yet turned up, and we now learn that the three others (who went with him), have not returned to their respective companies. When I was in that Brigade dug-out last night the M.O. casually remarked to me that he had attended to four officers, who appeared to belong to our brigade, at about 6 in the evening. They were all wounded; one was very bad. In the light of the present situation it certainly looks as if they must have been the unfortunate four. So Captain Andrews has sent Giffin down there to in-quire. It looks serious.

It is now 6 p.m. I must close. Captain Andrews says that I had better warn you that you must not expect letters very frequently now, as it is not easy to get them off from here. We are going further up to-night. But do not worry; it is as safe there as here!

A postscript to this letter states: "It is as I surmised. Hal-stead, Barker, Ronald, and Wood are all wounded—by the same shell."

The *Lancashire Fusiliers' Annual* thus sums up the events of July 1 and the fate of these four officers:

On July 1st, the Battalion returned to the forward area. We were to have gone into our old billets in the Prison and the Magazine, but, as a 17in. shell had just landed in the Magazine and the foundations of the Prison had been shaken by 8in. duds, it was impossible to do so. Half the Battalion therefore found billets in the Ramparts, etc., the other half and Headquarters went back to Goldfish Château. During the afternoon of July 1, the Battalion suffered the most severe loss it had suffered for some time. Four officers, Lieut. W. C. Ronald, Lieutenant H. A. Wood, Lieutenant J. Halstead and Second-Lieutenant H. A. Barker, one officer from each Company, had started up to reconnoitre the line. At Wells Cross Roads a shell landed and wounded all four. Second-Lieutenant Barker died of his wounds a month later, but the other three have all recovered.

The Lancashire Fusiliers' Annual goes on to say that "On July 2nd the Battalion moved up into the Potijze sector. We had a hot reception, the enemy sent over 1,500 shells all round Battalion Headquarters between midnight and 5 a.m." But, as the following extract from my diary will show, the move took place while I was otherwise engaged:

JULY 2ND. There came an order for a working party of one officer and twenty men to report at Potijze dump at once. So Captain Andrew detailed me to take Sergeant Baldwin and twenty men of 5 Platoon. We went by the Water-pipe track across the open, in broad daylight. Enemy observation balloons were up all the time and spotted us. A few shells were fired, but nobody was hit.

When we got to Potijze the men were given material to take to Pagoda Trench; so we proceeded there in small parties. We got to Pagoda Trench at 7.30; but enemy observation balloons were still up, and a few bullets whizzed over the trench, so it was not yet safe to work. We accordingly sat in the trench and waited. Darkness fell upon a beautiful summer evening before the observation balloons disappeared. At 9.30 we decided that it was safe to begin work. The work to be done consisted of repairing duck-boards. It did not require much supervising, especially as representatives of the Royal Engineers were managing it, so Baldwin and I sat down and chatted most of the time. As a matter of fact, we had six men too many; so they had nothing to do.

One or two machine-gun and rifle bullets whizzed past while we were there, but no one was hit. We stopped at 11.30 and filed back down the communication trench through Potijze Wood. Coming round the corner here—near Bottle Wall—we were shelled rather badly; the shells were bursting very near us—one within six yards—but none of my party were hit. An R.E. officer close by was wounded.

We got back to Potijze dump at 12 midnight. I reported to Captain Andrews, who was there in a dug-out. The Company had moved up while we had been on this working party. I saw my party into their new dug-outs here, and then came back and spent the night in the officers' dug-out at Potijze with Captain Andrews, Giffin, and Gratton. Allen was with a working party and did not return until 3 a. m....

Shells were falling round our dug-out all night. One shell blew a dug-out, a few yards away, to pieces, killing two, wounding two, and causing shell-shock to the remaining man—all of 5 Platoon (Allen's platoon). Two more B Company men were wounded on fatigue near St. Jean. A good many transport men and horses, and men of other units, were killed and wounded near. It was what might be called a rough night in the Ypres Salient! Morning (July 3) dawned bright and clear.

A message came to us at 5 a.m. that I must proceed to Bilge Trench to be temporarily attached to D Company in Wood's place. At present C Company (Captain Mordecai) are in the front line, with their headquarters in the Estaminet (the deep tunnel dug-out beneath

Wieltje). D Company (Captain Bodington) are in support in Bilge Trench. Colonel Best-Dunkley calls it the front line, and considers it such in his dispositions. A Company (Captain Briggs) are in reserve. And B Company (Captain Andrews) are in Potijze dug-outs. Battalion Headquarters are close to Potijze.

CHAPTER 9

Bilge Trench

When I got to Bilge Trench I found that the facilities for letter-writing were not quite what they had been before. But there was plenty to write about. Every hour one was confronted with some new aspect of modern warfare. I had an interesting taste of it in Bilge Trench and its vicinity! On July 5 I began a letter home in the following tone: "Letter-writing of the proper kind is becoming quite a problem. I am quite behind-hand, but fortunately I am keeping lengthy diary notes in pencil; so, if I have not the time to let you know all my experiences just now, I hope to get a connected narrative together sometime. How ripping it will be when that far-off day arrives when I can come home and tell you all about everything! It will be a long tale which I shall have to tell. I have almost forgotten which articles from home I have acknowledged and which not. I received a nice parcel the other day, containing a cake which we had for tea in the mess and which was duly appreciated—also chocolates, toffee, ink, socks, and badge...." As this letter intimates, the diary tells the clearest story at this period. So for the time being I will quote from the diary:

July 3rd. I left Potijze at 7.20 a.m. accompanied by a runner named Firth. We passed A Company in Garden Street on the way. I saw Captain Briggs, Hickey, Kerr, and Walsh. They have had no casualties yet. We arrived in Bilge Trench at 8 a.m. Here I found Captain Bodington, Victor Telfer, and Beesley. I had a cup of tea and a sleep during the morning. In the afternoon I sent for my batman, Critchley, as I expected to be here some days. He brought up some letters for me.... In the evening Captain Blamey returned from leave, and so takes over command of D Company. At 10.30 p.m. Beesley went out into no man's land with a patrol; and Kerr, of A Company, Telfer, and I went out on a wiring party just behind him. We went up Durham Trench by ourselves first; the party followed on after. Machine-gun bullets whizzed past the desolate area; it was not exactly pleasant. We went on along New Garden Street, and waited for the parties. Then they drew wire and pickets which had been dumped by a carrying party under Giffin. The Brigade-Major and Colonel Best-Dunkley went past us while we were at this spot. We were delayed some time. Then we moved on and got into Hopkins Trench, a new trench pushed out right beyond our front line. They began to get over the top here, but made a great row about it. Naturally the enemy heard us and a hell of a strafe began. It continued for about five minutes; then we got on again. Beesley's covering party was right out in front of a hedge in no man's land. Our men started wiring in front of Hopkins Trench, and just behind the hedge. Things seem very weird out there; from the continual series of Véry lights it looks just as if the enemy trenches were stretched all around one. While we were there a little raid took place on our left. At times machine-guns fired across from both sides—not exactly pleasant for us in the middle of it all!

July 4th. We returned to Bilge Trench about 2 a.m. I had a sleep in my clothes until 8. Then breakfast. Then a wash and shave. I was officer of the watch during the morning. Duty consists of seeing that sentries are at their posts, and fatigue parties at work. Hostile aircraft frequently comes over and fires machine-gun bullets down into the trenches. Our guns fire shrapnel at them, but I have not yet seen one hit. Periodical shelling continues all day. At present the Germans continue to drop shell after shell on one spot near St. Jean behind us. They scream over us and alight on the same spot every time.

In the afternoon I had a chat with Telfer and Beesley, and then an hour's sleep. Then tea. After tea Beesley and I went up Durham Trench to Wieltje—the strong point on our front line at present held by C Company. The headquarters of a company of the 1/4th King's Own Royal Lancaster Regiment is also down in the mine at Wieltje. We went down here and saw Captain Mordecai, Agnew, and Verity. The first had a bloody bandage round his head; he has been wounded by a piece of shrapnel, but is not bad enough to get away. We stayed there a few minutes and then went into Dead End, the front line trench. Here we saw Francis (who was at Scarborough before I came out, and who has just come back here again. He was wounded out here in January in this unit) and Walsh and I sat and had a chat with them there. These trenches are very pretty—the parapet and parados covered with grass and flowers. In fact they seem to have become natural features in the geography of the district.

We returned via New John Street to our Company Headquarters in Bilge Trench for dinner. At 9.30 I went with Captain Blamey for a stroll up Durham Trench, Armitage Trench and Hopkins Trench, out into no man's land. Blamey was not sure of the geography of this particular part and wanted to have a look round; so I went with him. Then Beesley got his patrol out again. Blamey and I then supervised a working party in Durham Trench.

JULY 5TH. All was moderately quiet until 1.50 a.m. Then we heard rifle shots, and more rifle shots, ringing out in no man's land; and at 2 a regular set-to began. The Cheshires on our immediate left were making a raid with an artillery barrage. It was quite a set-to. Beesley got back in time. He, Telfer, and I watched it all from the parapet of Durham Trench. The enemy were too preoccupied to trouble to shoot us! This went on for about half an hour. Then the enemy retaliated in a furious manner with his artillery. We made for Wieltje dug-out and were only just in time. Shells were falling everywhere in a continual succession. It was a terrific bombardment; it was the biggest row I have heard since the Battle of Messines! After a few minutes we went and sat in C Company dug-out in the Estaminet. Captain Andrews was there too. Who should walk in but Gaulter, of Hut 5 at Gailes! He is in the 1/4th King's Own in our Brigade. I had a talk with him. We returned about 4 a.m. to Bilge Trench; and Andrews went back to Potijze.

When we got back to Bilge Trench we found that there had been two or three casualties, and one dug-out totally demolished. Colonel Best-Dunkley came on the scene, and started strafing one or two people about something. He stayed and had a cup of tea in our mess. He asked me whether I could tell him what were the six infantry regiments, including the Lancashire Fusiliers, which took part in the Battle of Minden! I confessed that I did not know. 'That's very feeble for a historian like you,' he said, with a blink. As a matter of fact, he could not think of all the names himself; he knew of about four.

The Colonel departed about 5 a.m. I then came on duty as officer of the watch until breakfast. The Germans were still shelling that spot near St. Jean—some of the nose-caps returned as far back as Bilge Trench. Sleep in the morning. There was a heavy bombardment of our trench from 12.20 to 12.45; one or two casualties. The padre called in to see us and had tea in our dugout. I had a little sleep before dinner, and was officer of the watch from 9 p.m. to 12 midnight. While on duty, I supervised a working party, consisting of Sergeant Dawson and eleven B Company men, in Bilge Trench. They were putting up camouflage. Sergeant Dawson tells me that Sergeant Butterworth is wounded. They have been having a hot time of it.

JULY 6TH. At 12 I had another sleep until 4 a.m., when I became officer of the watch again. There was a good deal of aircraft about. One aeroplane, despite the fact that shrapnel was fired at it every time, was very persevering in returning over and over again. I felt horribly sleepy all the time. At 7.30 Sergeant-Major Stanton took over duty again. So I had my breakfast. Then I had another sleep. At midday I was awakened hearing great excitement occasioned by an air scrap overhead. Four were brought down. I felt too cosy to trouble to get up and look! Up at 12.45. One or two whizz-bangs landed uncomfortably near while I was shaving. At 2 p.m. there was another air scrap overhead. We watched it through our glasses. We saw one of our aeroplanes cut off and brought down into the Boche lines completely smashed. Then one of the German aeroplanes was brought down. There has been considerable aerial activity all day.

JULY 7TH. On patrol with Beesley at night (July 6–7). We left our own trench soon after 10 p.m. and filed up the communication trench and out into no man's land. The moon was shining brightly and a good deal of country was visible in its silvery light. We got our patrol stationed along the line of a hedge, facing the German front line. Then we crouched along to the left to get into touch with a patrol sent out by the Cheshires on our left. It was a strange sensation creeping along no man's land, grasping our revolvers, and anxiously peering into every hedge or bush or tuft of grass or ruined cottage (such as Argyle Farm and Lytham Cot) wondering whether it were occupied; and ever and anon gingerly glancing in the direction of the German trenches, wondering whether we were seen! I cannot understand why we were not sniped; logically we ought to have been; but, fortunately, the enemy were not logical on this occasion.

We found the party of the Cheshires and then crept back. We were walking over the same ground where the recent bombing raid had taken place. I am glad the enemy did not do a stunt while we were there! Kerr and Telfer were behind us, wiring. Our patrol, or covering party, ran right across what was *avant la guerre*, the St. Julien Road. It is now so completely overgrown with grass that it is scarcely distinguishable at first sight from the remaining country in no man's land. All went well until 12.30 a.m. But for the rumble of the guns on both sides of us and the periodical sound of the shells flying high over our heads, the Véry lights and the occasional rat-tat of a machine-gun, there was little in the peaceful, moonlit country-side to suggest to us the fact that we were between our own lines and those of the enemy!

However, at 12.30 a.m. we received a curt reminder that there was a war on, and that we were in the very heart of it. Captain Blamey had given orders that, since I was to be officer of the watch in our trench at 4 in the morning, I must leave the patrol party at 12.30 and return in order to be able to get a little sleep before going on duty; so Beesley said that as it was now 12.30 I had better go; and I, therefore, stealthily made my departure. A few yards behind were the wiring party; so I whispered a word or two to Kerr and Telfer. Telfer said that I ought to have a man with me; one is not supposed to go about here alone; so he detailed a man. We were just setting off when, like a bolt from the blue, a rifle bomb burst right amongst the wiring party with a crack; and immediately we heard groans. Three men were wounded: one had his leg very badly smashed, and the other two had nice 'Blighties'—one in the leg, the other in the nose.

That was the first shot. Shell followed shell and bomb followed bomb in one continuous succession; a regular strafe began. We made a bound for the nearest trench (Hopkins Trench) behind us. The bottom was full of water; that did not matter; in we splashed, and only just in time. The shells were dropping everywhere. An aeroplane flew overhead and dropped a few bombs, just to liven things up a little more! And then a machine-gun also opened right on to us—only the parapet of the little trench saved us. But for this trench we would all have been wiped out; the bullets were peppering the parapet. Such a to-do it was! After about ten minutes of this, Kerr said that I had better go.

Then began the most desperate adventure I have so far struck. I made a dash across the open into the communication trench and hurried down it, bent double. I had to duck constantly, for shells were bursting around me every yard of the journey. The dust raised by the explosions enveloped me; and, to crown all, gas shells came over. But I did not trouble to put my box-respirator on; the gas was not so bad as that. I simply dashed from bay to bay, crouching behind each traverse as the shells or bombs exploded and then bounding on to the next. In many places I went down into thick mud and water up to my knees; but when it is a question of life or death things like that do not trouble one.

At last I reached Bilge Trench in safety. It was crowded with fugitives from working parties—amongst them many wounded men. There have been a whole crowd wounded and some, including Sergeant Fergusson of the patrol, gassed. Having got back, I reported the proceedings to Captain Blamey, and then went to sleep.

At 4 a.m. I got up again and went on duty as officer of the watch. Sergeant-Major Stanton relieved me at 7. Writing in the morning. Much aerial activity. Sleep in the afternoon until 7.30 p.m. Working party with Sergeant Noden in New John Street from Monmouth Trench to Dead End in the evening.

JULY 8TH. I have just received two letters from home—July 4 and July 5—and I am sorry to observe that you are both becoming anxious just because you have not heard from me for a day or two. You really must not do this. Circumstances may easily arise at any time out here which would prevent my writing for a week or two; it is absurd to put a bad construction on everything. I always write when I can. By the way, blotting paper would be a great aid to writing. But some is probably on the way by now. I received a parcel from home yesterday containing parkin, chocolates, socks, writing material, and magazines. Thank you very much indeed. They have been duly appreciated.

We had three artillery officers from the 36th Division here yesterday reconnoitring as to where to place their guns. They were at the Battle of Messines and are now coming up here. Recently we have had hardly any guns here; we have been biding our time; if we had had them here now the Germans would have found them out; as it is, they will come as a surprise upon the enemy now; he will not have time to locate them before the great push. We are having the same artillery which did the job at Messines.

I spent yesterday afternoon sleeping. At dinner I found that Second-Lieutenant Talbot Dickinson,

M.C., had returned from leave. He ought to have had his investiture while on leave, but, as there was not one fixed at Buckingham Palace until a few days after the date on which he should return, he had to come back without it.

Yesterday evening I was supervising a working party under Sergeant Noden, repairing the parapet of a trench. All was quiet while we were at it; but I knew that a raid, about a mile away on our right, was fixed for 1.30 this morning. So, my party having finished their job, I brought them away at 1.20 and got them all back in their dug-outs by 1.30. Then, just as I entered our Company Headquarters dug-out at 1.30, the peaceful night was suddenly turned into hell. With a thunderous noise shells came over from the German guns in hundreds. Our dug-outs seemed to be their particular mark. ('When in doubt, shell Bilge!' was a maxim which Bodington used to attribute to the enemy artillery opposite us.) The place shook. Captain Blamey, Captain Bodington, Beesley, Dickinson and I were inside. We began to think that the dug-out was going to be blown to atoms; but we occupied ourselves by eating some of the parkin you sent! The candles were twice blown out by the force of the exploding shells. It seemed impossible that anything could live in such a bombardment. After about ten minutes of this the others went out, saying that all the officers in the Company should not crowd in the same dug-out during a bombardment because if a shell were to blow the dug-out to pieces we would all be knocked out, which would not do; so Dickinson and I alone remained. I remarked to him that this was a pleasant welcome for him on his return from leave! After 2 a.m. the bombardment began to slacken down; and by 2.15 it was all over, and quiet reigned again. I noticed that it had begun to rain. When we took stock we found that D Company had not suffered a single casualty on this occasion! This struck me as being extraordinary when one takes into consideration the fact that our trench was simply packed like sardines with various returning working parties which had all got congested here—working parties from various companies and regiments; there were some Irish amongst them. It was amusing to listen to the language: men shouting, with all kinds of unmentionable oaths, to each other to get a 'bloody move on for —— sake!'

It is amusing what a number of new men, 'obviously Derbyites and conscripts,' as Beesley said the other day, have got the wind up. One incident of the kind, related by Captain Bodington, was very funny. He was walking along a trench last night and a man came rushing along as if the whole German Army were chasing him; and he bumped right into Bodington, nearly sending him flying. Bodington asked him whatever was the matter; and the man replied in a voice of abject terror, 'They're sniping at us up there, sir!'

At 2.30 this morning I retired to rest—in my clothes of course; we do not undress in the trenches. At 5.40 I rose and took on officer of the watch until breakfast at 8.45, when I was relieved by Sergeant-Major Stanton. It was raining, so I wore my trench-coat. After breakfast I retired to rest again. But at 10.15 I noticed something happen: our guns, of which we have heard so little during this week in the trenches, began to bombard the enemy lines. Not an intense bombardment, but a continuous and systematic bombardment; they have been at it all day with the exception of a pause for about an hour in the middle of the day. The German guns have been quiet all day since they ceased at 2.15 this morning. There is always a calm after a storm. It is fine again now. Well—cheerio!...

My diary of the same date (July 8) carries on:

Germans started shelling us at 7.45 p.m. Dinner. Sleep from 10 to 11.30. Then I went into Company Headquarters to be ready for chits, as all the other officers were away somewhere. The dug-out was shelled while I was in there; the candle was blown out once. The shells were landing pretty close.

JULY 9TH. Sleep 1 a.m. to 4.30. Officer of the watch from 4.30 to 8. Then breakfast. Sleep, or tried to, in the morning. The Germans were shelling Bilge Trench the whole time. Lunch at 1.30. Got down again after tea. Then, at 6 p.m., I left Bilge Trench with my batman Critchley and proceeded to Potijze to rejoin B Company, as D Company's tour in the front line is now concluded." Thus ended the memorable stay in Bilge Trench.

CHAPTER 10

The Ramparts

My diary of July 9 tells how we once again got back to the
cosy dug-outs in the Ramparts, those ramparts from whence
was continually stretched out before our ken, in sunshine and
in moonlight, the heart of the dead city.

When I arrived at Potijze:

> Allen had gone to the Ramparts to take over, as B
> Company proceeds there to-night. D Company are go-
> ing to Goldfish Château, the other side of Ypres. I had
> dinner at Potijze. Things were quite peaceful at that time;
> we stood outside after dinner and admired the view in
> the Salient. Just a few shells were flying over. At 11 p.m.
> Captain Andrews, Dickinson and I, with Sergeant-Ma-
> jor Preston and a few runners, left Potijze and returned
> to the dug-outs in the Ramparts. There is more room
> to move about here!

My first letter home after my return to the Rampart runs
as follows:

> JULY 10TH. I am now back with B Company, as D
> Company have come out of the trenches. Dickinson
> has been transferred from D Company and appointed
> second-in-command of B Company in Halstead's place;
> and he is to be in command of the Company in the
> push. Captain Andrews will be, in the push (not be-
> fore: Major Brighten is back and is on 'battle reserve!'),
> second-in-command to Colonel Best-Dunkley—the

man who stands by waiting for the other man to die,' as Colonel Balfour has wittily remarked to Captain Andrews upon the arrangement! Captain Andrews is really a very smart man; he could have been a staff officer once, but Colonel Best-Dunkley would not let him go in for it. He did not want to lose him. Colonel Hindle stands in a similar position to General Stockwell.

Gratton has gone to Headquarters (as Assistant Adjutant), so the officers in B Company Mess now are Captain Andrews, Dickinson, Giffin, Allen and myself, also an M.O. I had dinner in this dug-out and then wrote a letter or two. Things were moderately peaceful at dinner-time, and for an hour or two after. At 11 p.m., the relief having been carried out, Captain Andrews, Dickinson and I, with Sergeant-Major Preston and a few runners, proceeded to Battalion Headquarters, which are at a strong point a little nearer the line. Then we turned back and proceeded to the dug-outs where we were on July 1 and July 2. Allen had preceded us to take over, and Giffin was with a working party in the trenches. While we were on our way a deuce of a row began on the north; it was a German raid on our trenches. So we watched it all the way. We got along quite well until we were almost here. Then two shells burst just in front of us. But we managed to get in quite safely.

I am now in the same dug-out as Giffin and Allen. We did not get up until midday to-day. Giffin made himself quite unbearable, and eventually remarked that we would be having a scrap soon. 'Yes. I notice that you seem to have been trying to make yourself as objectionable as possible!' I dryly replied. He then declared that he was only pulling my leg, and he has not been quite so bad since then.

This afternoon we had platoon inspections. Sergeant Baldwin carried on with 7 Platoon. Then Giffin came on the scene and said that he wanted him in 8 Platoon because, since he is to go over the top with 8 Platoon he ought to be with them now in order to get to know the men. Now, as you know, Baldwin was in 7 Platoon as a corporal, so he naturally knows the men in 7 Platoon very well indeed; also, he himself prefers, I believe, to be in 7 Platoon; also, I want him as my platoon sergeant: three excellent arguments why he should remain, as Captain Andrews has ordered to-day. Giffin said that he would see Captain Andrews about it. Then we fell to discussing the matter. The cause of the controversy is really to be traced in a lack of sergeants now in B Company. The Quartermaster-Sergeant having been wounded, Sergeant Jack has taken his place; Sergeant Butterworth has been wounded; and Sergeant Williams and Sergeant Dawson are on 'battle reserve.' There, therefore, remain only three sergeants to four platoons; and all the N. C. O.'s in my platoon are lance-corporals and cannot, therefore, very well be promoted to sergeant at a bound....

I have since discussed the matter with Allen. He sees in the difficulty the chance of a solution which would give me what I want, and also secure something which he wants. At present he has got Sergeant —— as his platoon sergeant. He says that he would not go over the top with him for worlds; so he suggests that that sergeant should be put on 'battle reserve' in place of Sergeant Williams and Corporal Stokes be promoted platoon sergeant of 5 Platoon; that Sergeant Williams should take 8 Platoon; and that I should thus retain Sergeant Baldwin for 7 Platoon. Personally I think that would be quite a good solution of the problem. I hope it will, when put forward, meet with the approval of Captain Andrews.

JULY 10TH (LATER). I have won! Captain Andrews has just been into our dug-out to give us our orders as to working parties for to-night. Giffin brought up the question of the platoon sergeants, and Captain Andrews immediately replied: 'Oh, you will have to carry on with Sergeant Williams at present; Sergeant Baldwin is going to remain with his old platoon'—7 Platoon! Giffin then asked whether Sergeant Williams would be going over the top with him; Captain Andrews replied that it would probably end in his doing so. Anyhow, Sergeant Baldwin is now definitely appointed to 7 Platoon. That is satisfactory. I am also quite satisfied with my section commanders—Lance-Corporal Livesey (Bombers), Lance-Corporal Tipping (Riflemen), Lance-Corporal Topping (Lewis Gunners), and Lance-Corporal Segar (Rifle Grenadiers). The men in my platoon are practically the same as they were when I first had 7 Platoon. So things are now much more satisfactory. I hope they will continue so.

While here we are under direct orders from Brigade. The Brigade-Major has just been in with detail of working parties for this evening. I am to take Sergeant Clews and a party of thirty men to carry ammunition from one dump to another.

I must now close. It is nearly dinner-time. It is 7.20 now; dinner at 7.30. I start with my party at 9.25.

My diary of July 10 states:

Working party in the evening with Sergeant Clews—carrying ammunition from a dump near White Château to a Brigade dump further on to the left, behind Congreve Walk. A very quiet night.

Next day I wrote home as follows:

JULY 11TH. We had Major Brighten and Captain Blamey in for dinner yesterday evening. Major Brighten is delightfully optimistic; he is, like Captain Andrews, positive that the war will be all over by October. He thinks that the coming offensive will settle the dispute. We discussed the war, its duration, and the coming battle. The other day I remarked to Captain Blamey that a landing ought, during the heat of the action, to be effected at a certain place, and that a certain famous General would probably be chosen to do it, because he has already done it (but under easier conditions!) on a former occasion. A day or two later Captain Blamey was astonished to receive information from Major Brighten that the very thing I had proposed, and by the very General I had suggested, was going to be done! So he told him that I had said that this General would probably be the one, because he had done it before; but Major Brighten said that he did not think that he had done it before. Captain Blamey said that he did not argue the point because he was not sure himself, but he told me about it afterwards. I told him that this general certainly had done this thing, and referred him to a certain despatch of Lord French. So at dinner yesterday evening the subject was again brought up. Major Brighten said that he had forgotten that this general had done this thing before, but accepted my statement as correct.

Major Brighten went on to say that the Colonel had been debating in Headquarters Mess the question as to who was the countess whose garter Edward III picked up, and nobody knew, could I enlighten them? I replied that I recollected having read of the incident, but had forgotten the name of the countess!...

My diary proceeds—under date July 11:

Working party in the evening with Sergeant Clews. We drew tools at Potijze dump, proceeded up Strand, which has been badly knocked about by shells, and repaired the parapet and parados of the front line to left and right of Strand. The Germans sent over trench-mortars on our left (about ten yards to the right of Giffin's party) while we were at it. Nobody was hurt. Dickinson had a party further to my right. It is quite high ground up there, and the front line trench slopes down to the right; over the parados the open ground is much lower, dotted with trees; it looks quite quaint when a flare goes up. We left about 1 a.m. and returned via Strand, Oxford Road, Pagoda Wood and Potijze. Then along Track 4. A thick mist came on, and we very nearly lost our way; I was with my party just behind Dickinson's party. We managed to find our way in time. To bed, 3 a.m.

JULY 12TH. One shell during the morning so shook the place that my head bumped up and down on my pillow. Before we were up the Brigade-Major (Thompson) came to see Captain Andrews about working parties. Brigade are very pleased with our work, especially as the —— left their work unfinished, owing to wind up about trench-mortars!

Up 2 p.m. Platoon inspections. Then lunch. From the sound I should imagine that our preliminary bombardment for the forthcoming offensive is beginning. Our artillery here is sending a good deal of stuff over. At 6 p.m. I commenced a period of twenty-four hours as Orderly Officer. My main duty consists of seeing that the road outside is cleared after heavy shelling: for this object, Baldwin has a party permanently on the job.

CHAPTER 11

Mustard Oil

"On the night of July 12th we were treated to a new form of gas, 'mustard oil.' The two Companies billeted in Ypres suffered heavily, the casualties numbering 3 officers and 114 other ranks."

Thus the *Lancashire Fusiliers' Annual*. The following letter, which I wrote in the Ramparts, after alluding to the working party recorded at the end of the last chapter, describes that great bombardment of Ypres:

13TH JULY. On Wednesday evening (July 11) I had had a working party, with Sergeant Clews, in the front line. Dickinson had a party on my right. The work was: repair of parapet and parados knocked in by recent shelling. While we were at it the Germans sent over trench-mortars, a kind of shell which rises to a great height, looking like a burning snake, and then descends and pierces right into the earth, exploding underneath and sending the earth above it in all directions. The men all crouched against the parapet with a certain amount of wind up; but they were well to our left. Giffin, who had a party some distance to our left, said that they were about ten yards to his right. He and his party were covered with dirt when one of them exploded. Dickinson and I ceased work about 1 a.m. and returned. While returning, a thick mist came on. Dickinson's party was in front; my party following behind his. It was all we could do to keep in touch; and we almost lost the way. The party in front kept halting while Dickinson tried to find the way; then they would go on at a great speed, so much so that we had to run to catch up, floundering into shell-holes; the men were cursing and swearing, each thinking that he knew the way himself: on the whole it was a box-up; but, as usual, we got home all right eventually. No casualties—two days without any casualties!

To-day I am Orderly Officer. My period of duty began at 6 p.m. yesterday and continues until 6 p.m. to-day. My chief duty is to see that the road is repaired after shelling. There is a party permanently detailed for the job under Sergeant Baldwin; they do not go out at night because their working hours are from 4 to 9 in the afternoons.

Captain Blamey, Captain Bodington, Captain Briggs and Gratton were in for dinner yesterday evening. Gratton is now Assistant Adjutant at Headquarters. Every day Colonel Best-Dunkley goes to a certain house (Hasler House at St. Jean) which has an upstairs still left, and, through field-glasses, gazes at the front over which we shall have to advance. On these trips Gratton accompanies him, and has to take bearings and answer silly questions. He says that he is becoming most horribly bored with it all. While they were at it yesterday a shell exploded just by them. Gratton says that he jumped down below as soon as he heard it come; he was hit by one or two bricks and covered with dirt; when he looked round again he expected to find the Colonel done in, but found him safe and sound!

Yesterday evening Captain Andrews, Giffin, Dickinson and Allen all went out on working parties. I remained behind as Orderly Officer. Captain Briggs and Gratton remained in my dug-out with me. After a while Gratton had to go to Brigade Headquarters next door to discuss a map with the Brigade-Major. Soon after he had left us—about 10.10 p.m.—a terrific shelling of the city began. Shells were bursting everywhere; the ground frequently vibrated as if mines were going off; dumps were blown up; and very soon parts of the city were in flames. It was a sight such as I have never seen before; at times the whole scene was as light as day; the flames encircled the already ruined and broken houses, bringing them to the ground with a rumbling crash. It was a grand and awful sight—a firework display better than any at Belle Vue, and free of charge! The sky was perforated with brilliant yellow light, and the shells were whizzing and crashing all round. The air was thick with sulphur. So much so that we did not smell something much more serious than sulphur. Amidst all the turmoil little gas-shells were exploding all over. As we could not smell the gas we did not take any notice of it. We little dreamt what the results were going to be. We knew not what a revelation the morrow had in store for us!

At about midnight I went to bed, and at about 6 this morning I heard Giffin returning from his working party. He was muttering something about gas and saying that he would be going sick with it in a few days, but I was too sleepy to take much notice. I rose at 10.30 and made my personal reconnaissance of the road, but only found two very serious shell-holes actually on the road. These I pointed out to Sergeant Baldwin and got his men at them. Then I began to hear things about gas. I saw Corporal Flint (our gas N. C. O.!) being led by Sergeant Donovan and Corporal Livesey in a very bad state; he could hardly walk, his eyes were streaming, and he was moaning that he had lost his eyesight. So I began to inquire as to what was the matter. I was then informed that there had been a whole lot of men gassed. Then Captain Andrews sent for me and questioned me about gas last night. I told him frankly that I had not smelt any. He said that it was very strange, because when he got back early this morning 'the place simply stank of it.' He said that there would be a devil of a row about it; there were about ten casualties already! But, as time went on, the numbers began to grow rapidly. Yet I had not smelt it; the sentry had not smelt it; and the Sergeant-Major had not smelt it! After some time the Colonel appeared on the scene. He informed us that A Company had got seventy-two casualties from last night's gas! (A Company were billeted in the Soap Factory, near the Cathedral.) We felt a little relieved, because we realized that ours was not the only company and by no means the worst; so we could not be held responsible, as we were fearing that we might be—myself in particular, as the only officer on the spot at the time, for not ordering box-respirators on. I, of course, never thought of ordering box-respirators, considering that I smelt no gas myself! The Colonel further told us that three officers in A Company—Walsh, Hickey, and Kerr—were suffering from gas. Hickey is very bad.

During the day our casualties have risen considerably. They are now twenty-eight, including Corporal Flint, Corporal Pendleton, Corporal Heap, Pritchard, Giffin's servant, and Critchley, my servant. There have been heavy casualties all over the city. The Boche has had a regular harvest if he only knew it! Over a thousand gas-casualties have been admitted to hospital from this city to-day. And many who have not yet reported sick are feeling bad. So much so that the Brigade-Major has agreed that all our working parties, but one small one under Allen, shall be cancelled for to-night. I feel all right. I must have a strong anti-gas constitution. This is a new kind of gas; the effects are delayed; but I do not think I am likely to get it now since I have hardly smelt any yet.

The Germans are doing the obvious thing—trying to prevent or hinder our forthcoming offensive. I notice that they have attacked near Nieuport and advanced to a depth of 600 yards on a 1400 yards front. I have been expecting an enemy attack here, because it is the best thing the Germans can do if they have any sense; and I have repeatedly said so, but have been told that I am silly, that the Germans dare not attack us because they are not strong enough. For a day I held the view that peace was coming in a week or two! But Bethmann-Hollweg's straightforward declaration that Germany will not make peace without annexations or indemnities, that she is out to conquer, has altered things. We now know exactly how we stand. Germany is still out for grab. Therefore she is far from beaten. *Ipso facto*, peace is out of the question. The end is not yet in sight. There is still a long struggle before us. I think the forthcoming battle here will be the semi-final: the final will be fought in the East about Christmas or the New Year. Constantinople still remains the key to victory, if victory is to be won by fighting.

My diary of July 13 concludes with the statement:

Captain Briggs's A Company—the remains of it— are coming to these billets to join with us. Gas casualties in Ypres (latest) over 3,000.

It was about this time (in the middle of July) that, in the course of one of my letters to my school-friend, Mr. K. L. P. Martin, then—having been rejected for service in the Army as medically unfit—a student at Manchester University, I had remarked that I would probably get a "Blighty" in a fortnight; and I would, therefore, want something interesting to read in hospital: would he please send me *England Since Waterloo*, by J. A. R. Marriott, whom I had heard lecturing at the Oxford Union on "The Problem of the Near East," in February, 1916, when I was a recruit in the 29th Royal Fusiliers?

Mr. Martin, who was staying with another friend, Mr. George Fasnacht, at Clayton Bridge, replied as follows:

The Hollies,
Clayton Bridge,
Manchester
July 23rd, 1917
Dear Floyd,

Many thanks for your last letter. So you consider that you are likely to become a casualty in the near future. I hope not. Though, if such an event should take place, I hope it will not be serious and will involve a sojourn in England for at least six months.

I will order the Marriott at once. I decline to accept it as off the debt I owe you. It will do as a twenty-first birthday present, as I have received no news re. Lovat Fraser. As soon as the book comes I will forward it on.

Teddy and myself had a glorious cycle ride yesterday. We rode to town, took the train to Ashley, then rode to Knutsford via Mobberley. At Knutsford we had tea and then proceeded to Pickmere where we had a row; then on to Great Budworth, Arley, Rostherne and Ashley. The country was glorious, a fine day, good roads, midsummer and Cheshire—the combination needs beating.

I may say that I am extremely pleased at Churchill going to the Ministry of Munitions.

Both Teddy and myself intend getting our photos taken this week, and I will forward copies of both to Middleton Junction.

Best wishes,
Yours,
Kenneth Martin

The Marriott was destined to have a curious history. As these pages will show, I got my "Blighty" in a fortnight all right. Meanwhile the book was on its way from England. It arrived after I had left the shores of France behind, me. I never received it. Kenneth Martin visited me in hospital at Worsley Hall in August and told me that he had sent it. I had to tell him that it had not reached me. When I returned to the Battalion in the spring of 1918, Padre Newman informed me that a book had come out for me after I had been wounded, that he had read it with much interest, and that it was now in the custody of Captain J. C. Latter, M.C. Latter was one of the original 2/5th officers who had been wounded in 1916 and who returned to the Battalion immediately after the Third Battle of Ypres, in August, 1917, and succeeded Reginald Andrews as Adjutant. But when Padre Newman told me this Captain A. H. G. Griggs, M.C., was Adjutant and Latter was away with Sir Herbert Plumer in Italy. However, Latter returned once more in the summer of 1918, and mentioned that he had a book belonging to me; but he disappeared again—first on to the Brigade Staff and then to a Staff job further away—as suddenly as he had reappeared. I did not see him again until we were both once more in civilian clothes, and I called at the Barracks at Bury one August afternoon in 1919. He again mentioned the Marriott, remarking that he had discovered it in his kit in August, 1917, and had not the faintest idea how it had got there!

117

CHAPTER 12

The City and the Trenches

After the bombardment of Ypres there still remained seven more days before our memorable nineteen days' sojourn in the ghastly Salient was to end. And memorable those days certainly were. Nearly every day brought with it some fresh adventure. For any boy who, like this boy, craved for excitement, and, while hating war theoretically and disliking it temperamentally, was not blind to the romance and grand drama of it all, there was ample satisfaction in the Great War; and perhaps on no other sector of the line did all the factors which are conducive to excitement obtain as they did in the dead city of the Salient and the shell-ploughed fields around it.

My diary of July 14 carries on as follows:

Up about 2 a.m. Twenty-eight more men in B Company reported sick with gas, but they were not sent to hospital. The M.O. said that they would be excused duty to-night and must report sick to-morrow morning. We had a little more gas in the afternoon. I think a German heavy exploded one of our own gas dumps near the Canal Bank. A dense cloud of vapour rose in that vicinity, and we felt the smell slowly drifting towards us in the almost breathless calm of a bright summer afternoon. Giffin, who was the senior officer present at the time, ordered respirators on. But it did not last long, so we went on with our tea.

In the evening Giffin and I were on a working party with Sergeant Clews, Sergeant Dawson and forty-five other ranks. We proceeded to Potijze Dump and drew tools; thence to Pagoda Trench and carried on with the making of a new trench branching off that trench. All went well for the first three quarters of an hour. Our guns were pounding the German trenches the whole time—the first preliminaries in the bombardment preceding our offensive. But the Germans do not always allow us to have all our own way in these matters; they always retaliate. And, by Jove, we did get some retaliation too! At 10.50 p.m. quite suddenly, a heavy shell exploded just near us; and a regular strafe commenced. I was standing near a shell-hole at the time, so I immediately crouched where I was; the men digging at the trench at once took refuge in the trench.

In a few minutes I mustered sufficient courage to make a dash for the trench. I got there just in time, for, soon afterwards, a shell burst almost where I had been. They were dropping all round us, both in front of and behind the trench. Only the trench could possibly have saved us. And it was a marvel that no one was hurt as it was. I honestly expected every moment to be my last; it was a miracle that none of our party were hit. If we had remained out in the open I firmly believe that the whole lot would have been knocked out. It seemed as if it was never going to cease.

I never went through such a disagreeable experience in my life before. Then, to crown all, gas shells began to be mixed with the others. There was soon a regular stink of gas; I smelt it this time all right. We got our respirators on, which added to our discomfort. This went on for quite a long time. Then it also began to pour with rain and we were all drenched. The night was pitch dark. Every now and then the exploding shells around us and far away, the burning dumps near Ypres and the star shells along the line, lit up the whole panorama with an effect like that of lightning. The water and mud grew thick in the trench; and still the shells fell thickly all around. We were thankful for the discomfort of rain because it saved us from being gassed.

JULY 15TH. About 1 a.m. Giffin decided, the shelling having slackened a little, that we had better get down a mine-shaft near; so we stumbled along to it in anything but a happy frame of mind. Everybody was cursing. Despite our discomfort, however, the humour of the situation under such circumstances cannot fail to strike one; I could not help chuckling. Eventually we got down the mine. It was horribly damp and dirty down there, but the atmosphere was much clearer; there was no smell of gas. That was a relief. And we felt much safer here! No heavies could reach us at such a depth as this. But it was all darkness. We remained in this subterranean sanctuary for three hours, standing on a water-covered floor, amidst dripping walls, in the darkness; above us, all the time, we could hear the dull thud and feel the vibration of the bursting shells. For want of anything better to pass the time away the men began to air their opinions about the war to each other. 'We're winning!' 'Are we heck as like; Billy's winning. Judging from t'newspapers you'd think t'war was over long since! They keep telling us he's beat; but they want to come out 'ere and see for 'emselves.... They say t'last seven years'll be t'worst!' Such was the conversation which was going on. Others had a sing-song. 'Hi-tiddle-ite! Take me back to Blighty; Blighty is the place for me!' rang out with great enthusiasm from the darkness underground.

When we did go upstairs again daylight had dawned. We left the mine at 4.20 a.m. Giffin went, with one or two men, back to the trench to replace the camouflage; he told me to get back to the Ramparts with the remainder as quickly as possible. I did so. We went along the road all the way from Potijze to Ypres. We were literally chased by gas-shells; we had to run in respirators as fast as we could go; we came round by the Menin Gate and got back into the Ramparts, safe and sound, about 4.45, very thankful that nobody in our party had got hurt. Other battalions out on working parties had had a good many casualties. One party of the King's Own had had one killed and eleven wounded by one shell on the Canal Bank.

When I got back to the Mess dug-out I found Captain Andrews, Dickinson, and Allen all sitting there. They had not been to bed. They had had a deuce of a time. The shells had been falling here as well—also the gas. But due precautions against gas had this time been taken! Captain Andrews declared that the rain had saved the lives of hundreds of men. Giffin got back soon after me. He is feeling the gas. We all got to bed about 6 a. m....

It was 3 in the afternoon when I got up. Before rising I read nine letters which were awaiting me—some post!

After describing the happenings of the previous night in a letter written home that Sunday afternoon I went on to say:

JULY 15TH. I shall pull through all these exciting little episodes all right. I am quite all right so far. Cheer up! Better times in store! We all look forward to that great day 'When war shall be no more.' It will be a glorious day when, at last, peace is attained. I am looking forward to the happy days to come and intend to have a good time then. We are now going through the storm. But there is a calm ahead: 'Peace shall follow battle, Night shall end in day.'

My diary of July 15 carries on:

In the evening I went on a working party with Allen. It was a case of extending the trench in Pagoda Wood another fifty yards. We set to work at 10 a.m. Our guns were bombarding the enemy trenches most of the time, but there were not many shells coming from the enemy. A few fell some hundred to two hundred yards away during the night. Our chief annoyance on this occasion was a German machine-gun firing from Kaiser Bill. It swept our trench completely. One man in my platoon, Berry by name, was wounded in the leg. It was a wonder there were no more casualties: the bullets were flying amongst us in great profusion. But they were mostly low, so not very dangerous. 'This is the place for "Blighties"!' Lance-Corporal Livesey encouragingly observed to me while they were whistling round us.

We stayed at the job quite a long time. I was beginning to wonder when Allen was going to pronounce it finished; the men were obviously fed up. At last he let half the party go at 2.30 a.m. and told me to take them back. We returned by the road all the way from Potijze to the Menin Gate. It was 3 a.m. when we got back to the Ramparts. It was getting quite light. Allen followed on with the remainder about half an hour later; he came through the fields. We had some refreshment and then went to bed.

JULY 16TH. I did not get up until 3 p.m. this afternoon. Since 8 Platoon has practically ceased to exist owing to gas casualties, 7 and 8 are again combined under Giffin, and I am second-in-command. Baldwin remains platoon sergeant. If and when we get sufficient reinforcements the two platoons will separate again.

The Germans have been bombarding Poperinghe with very big shells to-day. The shops, I hear, are all shut. It looks as if they intend to destroy the town. Our great bombardment of the enemy trenches is in progress.

That evening I wrote a lengthy letter home. In the course of it I said:

JULY 16TH. The padre is in hospital at present, having been wounded by a shell in the streets of the city the other day. It is only a very slight wound, so he will not be in hospital long. With regard to the four officers who were wounded on July 1—Ronald is in hospital in Bristol doing well; Halstead, with a wound in the stomach, is going to 'Blighty' shortly; Barker and Wood are very bad indeed, the former was given up altogether the other day. They are much too bad to cross the water yet. We were all amused to read in the Manchester Guardian that Halstead had been lately in the Army Ordnance Corps; it is, of course, incorrect.

Whenever Colonel Best-Dunkley or Major Brighten come into our Mess they always ask me what I think of the war and when I think it is going to end. They came in yesterday. Colonel Best-Dunkley, with his customary squint and twitch of the nose (I have been told that he contracted this habit as the result of shell-shock on the Somme), said: 'Well, "General Floyd," what do you think of the war? How long is it going to last?' I replied: 'February, 1918.' They then always give vent to great amusement, especially when I mention Palestine; but I really think this sinister commanding officer is not at all badly disposed towards me; in fact I am inclined to think that he likes me! I do not dislike him at all.

I am Orderly Officer to-night so am now going to bed. The Germans are sending copious gas shells over while I am writing this, but we have got the gas curtain down in our dug-out and it has been sprayed; all precautions have been taken; so we ought to be all right. There is also a good deal of shelling of a heavier kind going on; our guns are giving the German trenches hell at present; we have kept up a consistent bombardment all day. The Germans are giving us some back now; but I feel quite safe in this dug-out! I am glad I am not on a working party to-night. So good night! Again I say, 'cheer up!' It's a funny world we live in!

My diary of July 17 states:

Up 11 a.m. Had breakfast while dressing. Reconnoitred the road; all correct. At 1.10 p.m. I reported to Captain Warburton at Brigade Headquarters about a working party for which I was detailed. Carberry, the Brigade bombing officer, explained to me what was to be done. At 1.30 I set off with a party of Sergeant Clews and thirty-four other ranks including Corporal Chamley and Lance-Corporal Topping. The job consisted of carrying boxes of bombs from a dump at the junction of Milner Walk and the road to White Château; then detonating bombs which were not already detonated; then carrying S.A.A. from one spot to another about twenty yards away. I left Corporal Chamley in charge of the first dump, where the men left their equipment. I went backwards and forwards myself. On one occasion, while I was at the junction of Milner Walk and the road, General Stockwell appeared. He asked me what we were doing; I told him; he expressed himself satisfied and proceeded up the trench. It was a very hot day and I felt very tired. My head began to ache. We finished at 5.30 p.m. Then we came back. Our guns were blazing away all day, making a great row. It was 6.30 when we got back to the Ramparts. I reported to Carberry at Brigade. I felt very bad indeed now. The exercise in the heat, after gas, was taking effect upon me. I did not have any dinner, but lay down. I was told that I looked white. I felt rotten. Giffin also is bad; he got some more gas last night. A good many more have reported sick with gas to-day. I think I have got a slight touch of it now. However, as the evening advanced I began to feel much better. By midnight I felt quite well again.

Next day I wrote home as follows:

JULY 18TH. More gas shells came over last night. We had the gas curtains down again, but, even so, gas is bound to get in. There are fresh gas casualties every day. The number is rising rapidly. Giffin has, at last, reported sick with gas and has departed to hospital to-day—another officer less! So now instead of having no platoon at all I find myself in command of the two, 7 and 8!

I never saw Lieutenant Giffin again. I shook hands with him in the dug-out and said good-bye when he announced that he had reported sick and was going down the line. He went away and never returned; I have heard absolutely nothing of him since.

Our guns have been blazing away all night, and are still pounding the enemy lines. Our bombardment is now going full swing. But the Germans are sending shells over too. Five B Company men were wounded by one shell, just outside, this morning. One of them was Hartshorne. He has got four shrapnel wounds and is off to hospital. I have been speaking to him this afternoon. He said that they were hurting a little, but he seemed quite happy about it. He said that he wished he was in hospital in Middleton! It is nothing very serious; it should prove a nice 'Blighty' case!

The padre is now back from hospital! He has not been there long, has he?

A few of those men who went to hospital with gas on July 13 were marked for 'Blighty' and were just off, when General Jeudwine stopped them and said that as few as possible from this Division must be sent home at present. So, instead of going back, they have turned up here again as 'fit.' Hard luck!

My diary of the same date (July 18) states that in the afternoon:

I went on a working party with Sergeant Clews and

fifteen men. We were filling in shell-holes on the road near St. Jean. After we had filled in a few we got shelled. We took refuge behind an artillery dug-out for about an hour. The shells were falling close all the time. One fell less than six yards from me. I quite thought we were going to have some casualties, but the only one we had was one man who got a scratch in the arm with a piece of shrapnel.

At 5.15 we decided to come back via a trench, as the shelling was still going on. All got back safely. But it is most disconcerting—one cannot go out on a little job like that in the afternoon without having the wind put up us vertical! I had tea and dinner. Then to bed. I felt very hot and could not get to sleep. Allen returned from a working party at 10.15 p.m. There was a strafe on at 10.30; the German trenches were being raided in four places.

The following day, I wrote to my mother as follows:

July 19th. I got up at 2.30 a.m. this morning, and with Sergeant Clews's working party filled in the remaining shell-holes (outside Hasler House). We had a moderately quiet time. Only about three shells burst anywhere near us the whole time. Yet we were working in broad daylight! We got back at 5.45 and I then went to bed again. I had breakfast in bed. Then some post arrived: a letter from Father dated July 16 and the enclosed from Norman Floyd. As I expected, he, too, is now in the Army; has been for some months. He is in the 74th Training Reserve Battalion, and is thinking of going in for a commission. I have advised him to do so—in a letter which I have just written to him.

I got up at midday and had lunch. The afternoon I took easy. The padre was in for tea. While we were having tea newspapers arrived. Captain Andrews opened the Daily Mail and exclaimed with horror:

'Good heavens! Churchill's been appointed Minister of Munitions!'

'Hurrah!' I exclaimed, nearly tumbling off my seat in my excitement.

'Good God! How awful!' dolefully exclaimed the padre, looking at me in amazement that I should express satisfaction at such a catastrophe. 'What? Are you pleased to hear that Churchill is in office again?' inquired he and Dickinson in surprise!

'Rather! he's one of our two most brilliant statesmen,' I replied.

Thereupon an argument began and continued throughout tea. I must say I never admired Lloyd George more than I do at this moment when, in face of most bitter public opposition, he has had the courage to give office to Churchill. I admire him for it.

The new appointments are certainly of a sensational nature. Carson leaves the Admiralty and enters the War Cabinet as Minister of Reconstruction (whatever that may mean!). Montagu becomes Secretary of State for India in Austen Chamberlain's place. Then the most startling thing of all—the wonderful Sir Eric Geddes becomes First Lord of the Admiralty! That is very significant indeed. The appointment of that extraordinary production of the war to the Admiralty at this particular moment is not, I think, unconnected with the forthcoming operations. I leave you to surmise what I mean. Churchill has now once more set foot upon the ladder, despite popular prejudice. Watch him now. He will not rest until he has mounted to the top. It is really delightful. How angry everybody will be! Do, please, pull their legs about it for me! But watch also Sir Eric Geddes. He is one of the most remarkable men of our time—general, admiral, statesman!

I am rather amused at the change in the Royal Name: our Royal Family is now to be known as the

Royal House of Windsor! It does strike me as pandering somewhat to popular prejudice. That King George should change his name to Windsor cannot change the fact of his ancestry; he is still a member of the Royal House of Coburg, to which King Albert of Belgium and King Manoel of Portugal belong: no legal document can alter the facts of heredity! not that I think any the worse of him because he is a Coburg. However, the Royal House of Windsor will be peculiarly the British Royal Family and will probably marry amongst the British nobility. To that I have no objection whatever, as I have said before.

No, I have not seen the King or the Queen out here; but I knew that the Queen was inspecting the hospitals in the town where we get off the train for this part of the front.

Talking of hospitals—the Padre says that Barker is not expected to live many hours longer. The other three are pulling through. We have got another officer gas casualty to-day. Kerr, who has been suffering from the effects of gas ever since July 12, has reported sick to-day and has gone to hospital for a fortnight. One by one we diminish! I feel quite all right.

I was talking to Sergeant Brogden—the new gas N. C. O.—last night. He comes from Middleton Junction. He says that he was in the Church Lads Brigade at St. Gabriel's.

I have been reading the leading article about popular scapegoats in the Church Times, and I agree with it. I think the young Duke of Argyll's attack on Archbishop Davidson in the Sunday Herald was conspicuous rather for venom than for good taste.

Earl Curzon's speech in the Lords on Mesopotamia I thought very sober and statesmanlike indeed. I read it in the Times.

The next day I wrote home as follows:

JULY 20TH. We actually had no working parties to take last night. How considerate of the Brigade-Major! So we had a good night's sleep. And we have not done anything particular to-day. We are going to have a change at last. After twenty days in the line we are going out to-night, and are going to have a few days in a rest camp some distance behind. The place to which we are going on this occasion is nothing like as far back as we were last month; but I can assure you it is a perfectly safe distance. So you need not worry. I can tell you it has been some twenty days! I have never experienced such a twenty days before; and I am glad to be looking back upon them, writing during the last few hours, rather than at the beginning. We are all glad to be going out again. General Stockwell has ordered that we have three days' complete rest; and Sir Hubert Gough has issued an order that on no account are the men in his Army to be worked more than four hours per day, inclusive of marching to and from parade ground, while out of the line. So the prospect is bright. It is now 4.10, and we are going to have tea. Our bombardment is still making a great row.

My diary of the same date (July 20) states:

At 4.30 p.m. Captain Briggs, Dickinson, Allen, Sergeant Donovan and I walked via Wells Cross Roads, La Brique (where our guns were very close together, their sound almost deafening us as we passed them), to Liverpool Trench. Here we reconnoitred our starting points for the forthcoming push. Then Allen and I went on with Sergeant Donovan up Threadneedle Street to Bilge Trench. We watched, through glasses, the German line going up in smoke. In present-day warfare I certainly think that artillery is the most formidable arm of the Service; it is artillery which is the chief factor deciding success or failure in all the great battles in the West. It is even now preparing the way for us. After having had a look round from over the parapet in Bilge Trench we returned the same way we had come; and we actually got safely back to the Ramparts without having any adventures whatever!

When we got back to the Ramparts our tour in the line was at an end. All we had to do now was await the arrival of relief. And a very pleasant sensation, indeed, that is to weary soldiers! The sensation of "relief" is the happiest of all the various sensations one had "out there." There were just a few hours of irritating expectancy to live through—followed sometimes, as at Givenchy in 1918, by some boring experience such as a "stand to" in some particular, and generally uninviting, positions—and then one would be free, safe and in a position and condition to enjoy a delightful sleep: free and safe for a few days, until the all too soon moment for return should come!

CHAPTER 13

Relief

My diary of July 20 goes on to state how our relief was effected:

We were relieved by a company of the 1/5th South Lancashires of General Lewis' 166 Brigade at 8.45 p.m. So I set off with my platoon at 9 p. m.... We went round Salvation Corner and across various tracks—a very roundabout way; but Sergeant Baldwin, Sergeant Dawson and I between us managed to find our way to Vlamertinghe somehow. Then we went along the road to Brandhoek Cross Roads and thence into our destination, B Camp, on the right.

The letter which I wrote home the next day describes the events of the two days in greater detail without naming places. It begins where my letter of the previous day left off, at tea-time:

JULY 21ST. After tea yesterday I went up to the trenches to reconnoitre our own positions as they will be on 'the day,' and the front over which we shall have to advance. I was accompanied by Allen and others. We got there and back again without any adventures whatever; but we saw crowds of batteries bombarding the German lines. The noise as we passed them was deafening. And through our glasses we saw the German lines going up in smoke. If the artillery fails to achieve exactly what the General orders the infantry is foredoomed to failure; and, conversely, if the artillery is successful the infantry ought to have things all plain sailing. That was the secret of the victory of Messines last month. Churchill, with his customary intelligence, has aptly summed up the matter in the following words: 'In this war two crude facts leap to the eye. The artillery kills. The infantry is killed. From this arises the obvious conclusion—the artillery at its maximum and infantry at its minimum.'

We got back at 6.45 and had dinner. At 8.30 we began to be relieved. So, at 9, I got off with my platoon. We had no adventures except that even the three of us—Sergeant Baldwin, Sergeant Dawson and I—had some difficulty in finding our way through the various tracks across the fields! We passed some simply huge field-guns firing into the enemy lines. On one occasion if I had not called out to inquire whether all was safe I would have been blown up with others by one of our own big guns. 'Just a minute,' was the reply; and then a loud report nearly lifted us off our feet as the shell left the muzzle of the gun which was pointing across the path we were taking! They ought to have had a picket out to warn passers-by as is done in the case of most big guns when firing.

We eventually got to our destination, a certain camp. We stayed the night there. We tried to get some sleep on the floor in a large elephant dug-out, but found it utterly impossible: the sound of the guns all round was too terrific. This bombardment is as yet only in its early stages. I was only a few hundred yards away from where I was last night on that night previous to the night of the Battle of Messines when the preliminary bombardment for that battle was at its height; yet I may say that the present one sounded last night just like that one sounded then. So what will it become as the days roll on?

We had breakfast at 4 this morning and marched off

from this camp at 6.40. We marched about nine miles to a village which was really only about six miles away! I can tell you I was, and we all were, very tired indeed when we got here. It was about midday when we arrived. We are still well in sound of the guns, but just nicely out of range of them. Nevertheless, air scraps have been going on overhead most of the day. We are under canvas—the whole battalion in a large field enclosed by hedges. The weather is splendid; fine camping weather. We had lunch about 2 p.m. Then I played a game something like tennis (badminton). The Colonel is very keen on it. When he saw that I was going to play he said, 'Oh, I'll back the "General,"' meaning me! Then he showed me how to play. He has been most agreeable with me all day. Major Brighten has started calling me 'The Field-Marshal!' I think I cause these gentlemen considerable amusement!

Sir Douglas Haig is in this village to-day; but as I have not been out of camp since I got here I have not seen anything of him.

CHAPTER 14

Watou

The time we spent at Valley Camp, Watou, is duly chronicled in my diary.

JULY 21ST. We got here at 12. Lunch at 2.... My servant Johnson reported sick with gas and departed for hospital; so I asked Sergeant Baldwin to suggest another. He took me to M'Connon. I endorsed the selection. Allen's servant, Parkinson, has also gone to hospital with gas to-day! To bed 10 p.m.

JULY 22ND (SUNDAY). Breakfast in bed. Up 9.30. The Colonel had a conference of all officers re training and man-power. Then there was a Church parade in the field at 12.15 p.m. The main points of the padre's sermon were Repentance, Hope, Intention. In the afternoon Dickinson and I went over my platoon roll with the Sergeant-Major (Preston) to see how we stand. He also did the same with the other platoons. After tea I had a walk into the village of Watou and purchased some chocolates. Then dinner. The padre tells me that Archbishop Lang is in Poperinghe to-day.

Critchley came back from hospital this evening; so he will resume his duties as my servant to-morrow.

Corporal Flint has died, in hospital, of gas.

JULY 23RD. Breakfast in bed. Up 7.30. Parade 8. Training during the morning. There were also lectures by company commanders on the forthcoming operations, and a lecture on the compass by Major Brighten. In the afternoon General Stockwell spoke about the forthcoming operations to all officers and N. C. O.'s. His speech was very interesting.... He is to have his Headquarters in Wieltje Dug-out. He said that casualties of this brigade while in Ypres this time had been 26 officers and 470 men. I have been very busy with matters relating to the push all day.

JULY 24TH. Battalion parade 8.30 a.m., followed by lectures on the forthcoming operations and a lecture to officers and N. C. O.'s on field messages by Major Brighten. In the afternoon platoons marched to Poperinghe to bathe at the Divisional Baths in the Square—just by the church, I left Valley Camp with my platoon at 1.45. We marched via St. Janster Biexen to Poperinghe and there bathed. Then I took my N. C. O.'s—Sergeant Baldwin, Corporal Livesey, Lance-Corporals Topping, Tipping, Heap and Hopkinson, and also Sergeant Dawson, to see a model of the battlefield at the Divisional School. We were ages finding it. We went the wrong way. But we eventually went along the Switch Road and found it. It was 6 p.m. by then. So I gave Baldwin, Topping, Tipping and Heap a pass to have tea in Poperinghe. Dawson and Hopkinson did not want one, so they set off back. I went into Poperinghe and had a drink of citron. I felt very tired. Then I set off back to Watou. I came across Dickinson returning on horseback. Then I caught up Sergeant Dawson and Lance-Corporal Hopkinson; and we got on a lorry which took us right as far as St. Janster Biexen. We then walked back to Valley Camp. I had dinner. Then to bed, feeling a little seedy.

JULY 25TH. Breakfast in bed at 8. Dickinson, feeling very bad, stayed in bed. I also felt washed out. I expect it is the gas at last taking effect. At 10 a.m. I set off with one officer and one N.C.O. from each company to reconnoitre the route to Query Camp. Beesley and I with Sergeant Clews and Sergeant Malone went one way; the others went another way. We found ourselves wrong, but eventually got right. It was raining, the route was thick with mud, and I felt very weary. I soon felt done to the world. We had some coffee in a hut on the Poperinghe road, about a mile from the town; then walked on to the Switch Road, right along that and on to the main Poperinghe-Vlamertinghe road. Here Beesley and his sergeant went one way and Sergeant Clews and I went another—right along the main road. We had a drink of citron at a little hut named Villa Franca. Then we turned to the left at Brandhoek Cross Roads, went through B Camp, and eventually reached Query Camp. I felt horribly fatigued and also had a most annoying cold.... Soon Beesley and his sergeant turned up. We had some citron in a cottage here. The Belgian woman who served us said that she had lost her father, mother and three brothers in the war. After this we went along Track 1 and back to the main road. Here we got a motor-lorry which took us through Poperinghe and right back to St. Janster Biexen. We walked back to Valley Camp from there. I really feel done up; and I have a headache in addition to my bad cold—something like influenza. All symptoms of gas! When we got back the rain had ceased and it was quite nice. A new large draft arrived about 6.30; there were two new officers with it—Richard Maxwell Barlow and Kenneth Leslie Smith. Young has also returned to the Battalion. There have been a number of drafts recently, so we are getting up strength again. Young, Barlow and Smith have all been posted to A Company; so, as the B and A Company Mess is joint, they mess with us.

The same day, I wrote home from Watou as follows:

JULY 25TH. Just a line to let you know that I have received all your letters up to July 20 and the parcel for which I thank you very much. I have been simply awfully busy—chiefly with maps and operation orders re coming offensive—and have not been able to write home during the last few days as a result. We are supposed to be resting, but I have hardly a moment to spare. General Stockwell lectured all officers and N. C. O.'s of this Battalion here in the field on Monday afternoon. He said that he was going to tell us everything that he knew himself about the coming battle, but did not tell us anything we did not already know! I do not think he told us all: if he did tell us all then I don't think much of the idea. The General had a cigarette in his mouth and his hands in his pockets the whole time he was speaking; he was quite jovial, cracking jokes all the time. He impressed upon us the importance of sending messages back when we reach our objectives; he said that if we do not do so it will mean his coming up to the front line himself for information 'and I don't want to have to do that,' he laughed, 'but it will come to that if necessary,' he went on in a more serious tone, 'and it will be woe betide the platoon commander whose negligence has brought his brigadier-general's life into danger!' At the conclusion of his speech the General asked whether any of us had any questions to ask. I could have asked one, but I know he would not have answered it; so I remained silent!

Archbishop Lang was in the big town half-way between here and the front line on Monday, but I did not see anything of him. Nor did I see the Queen when she was inspecting the hospitals there. But I think it very fine of Queen Mary to visit troops within range of the Germans guns as she did.

It is now evening and is quite bright, the sun is shining into the tent where I am writing this. We have been stationed here since July 21, and are now marching back in a few minutes to a camp beyond the above-mentioned town—where I went to reconnoitre this morning.

You will see that it is impossible to write any reply to 'Bumjo' at present as I have not the time. I also warn you not to get the wind up if you do not hear from me for a week or so. I can quite foresee a period of that length elapsing between my letters now, as before this present week is out we shall be engaged in fighting the great battle of the North. 'Bumjo' will have to wait until we come out of action again. I intend to deal with him and give him the telling-off which his impudence and his treason are asking for after the battle. I hope to have more leisure then! So *au revoir!*

These days at Watou, while being days full of work, were not unpleasant. We had plenty to talk about; and, seated on the grass on a summer evening, Joe Roake would make us rock with laughter at his quaint and humorous tales of his experiences when a sergeant at Loos and other battles. Roake was always a great asset to any mess when he honoured it by a visit. He hated Headquarters Mess; he was always ready to jump at any excuse to get away from the society of Colonel Best-Dunkley; and he was never happier than when, over a nice selection of drinks, he was retailing the Colonel's latest sayings and doings. And we, needless to say, were never happier than when listening to him on this most interesting topic! Roake and Humfrey with little "Darky," who was their invariable companion, were always welcome.

It was at this time that news came across that a son and heir had been born to Colonel Best-Dunkley. The event was one of considerable interest, and was widely discussed. "Poor little ——! To think that there's another Best-Dunkley in the world to look forward to!" exclaimed our humorous friend when he heard the news. "Well, when he grows up he will always have the gratification of knowing that his father was a colonel in the Great War!" mused Captain Andrews in a tone which suggested that he had a presentiment that Colonel Best-Dunkley would not survive the coming push. And, somehow—though nobody ever anticipated for a moment that he would win the V. C.—we all discussed the probability of his falling, and always thought that the odds were in favour of his falling. And to be perfectly frank (my object in writing this book is to tell the truth), nobody regretted the probability! If we had really known what kind of a man he was, if we had been able then to fathom beneath the forbidding externals, we might have felt very differently about it. But it is not given to man to know the future or even to discern the heart of his most intimate acquaintance! We only saw in him a man who was as unscrupulous as his prototype Napoleon in all matters which affected his own personal ambition, the petty tyrant of the parade ground, who could occasionally be very agreeable, but of whom all were afraid or suspicious, because none knew when his mood would change.

In a few days this man was going to give everybody who knew him the surprise of their lives. Had he any presentiment or intention as to the future himself? I think he had both intention and presentiment. Throughout the whole summer of 1917 his whole heart and soul were absorbed in preparation for the coming push; never did a man give his mind more completely, unstintingly, and whole-heartedly to a project than Best-Dunkley did to the Ypres offensive which was to have carried us to the Gravenstafel Ridge, then on to the Paschendaele Ridge, into Roulers and across the plains of Belgium.

He was determined to associate his name indelibly with the field of Ypres; he was determined to win the highest possible decoration on July 31: he knew what the risks were; he had seen enough of war to know what a modern push meant; he had not come through Guillemont and Ginchy for nothing and learnt nothing; he was determined to stake life and limbs and everything on the attainment of his ambition. He was determined to cover himself with glory; he was determined to let people see that he did not know what fear was. And I think—there was that in his bearing the nearer the day became which suggested it, everybody who had known him of old declaring that they noticed a certain change in him during the last two months of his life—that he felt that his glory would be purchased at the cost of his life.

I well remember one afternoon in the Ramparts when Captain Andrews came in and told us that it had been proposed that Major Brighten should take the Battalion over the top in the push and the Colonel remain behind on "battle reserve." Captain Andrews said that that would be fine, because if the push were a success—as it was sure to be—Major Brighten would probably get the D. S. O. before the Colonel, which would annoy the Colonel intensely; and he said that he would do anything, risk anything to bring success to our beloved Major Brighten—feelings which we all cordially reciprocated.

But Colonel Best-Dunkley would not hear of it. He implored the General to allow him to lead his battalion over the top; he waxed most importunate in his entreaties, almost bursting into tears at the thought of being debarred from going over with the Battalion; and, at last, his request was granted and the General agreed that Best-Dunkley should take the Battalion over.

Another very gallant officer was also very grieved when he was informed that he was detailed to be on "battle reserve" for the push. That officer was Kenneth Blamey. When Captain Blamey was informed that his second-in-command would take the Company over he implored to be allowed to go over the top with his company. But his request was not granted. Bodington was to take D Company over. It would not do for all company commanders to go over the top at once: the future has to be considered.

One more reminiscence before I close this chapter. It was at Watou that fat Joye used to come into the tent and get me to talk to him about the war. I remember him coming in to see us the last night at Watou and saying to me that we would both have nice "Blighties" in the leg in a few days. I replied that I hoped so. Things turned out exactly as Joye forecast: about ten days later I met him on the grand staircase in Worsley Hall!

CHAPTER 15

The Days Before

On the evening of July 25 the 164 Brigade marched back from the Watou area to the camps behind Ypres; we went to Query Camp. In my tent at Query Camp on July 27 I wrote my last letter home before going into action. It ran as follows:

> JULY 27TH. I have received all letters up to date: I got father's letter of July 23 this morning. I am still very busy, but have found time this afternoon to send a reply to 'Bumjo's' insolent letter to the Middleton Guardian and to write this.
>
> We left the last camp at 9.30 on the evening of July 25 and marched back here. We are now in a camp behind the line. We got here at 1 in the morning. Then we had dinner. A and B Companies mess in the same tent, so we had the two new officers—Barlow and Smith—who arrived just before we marched off from the other camp.... They have just come out from Scarborough.
>
> We went to bed at 2.20. Allen and I had a tent to ourselves, but were yesterday joined by Harwood, a new officer who arrived yesterday and has been posted to B Company. He seems all right. The new officers are all fresh from cadet battalions via Scarborough. Captain Cocrame, who has been at the Army School since June, has returned to-day, so our mess is increasing. A and B Company Mess now consists of Captain Briggs, Captain Cocrame, West, Barlow, Smith, Young, Dickinson,

Allen, Harwood and myself. Captain Andrews has gone to Headquarters.

The weather just now is glorious—too hot to move. Just by our tent there is a military railway constantly carrying things and men up to the front line. The engines and trucks are quaint little things. They have a bell which sounds like the trams running from Blackpool to Bispham and beyond. One expects to see the sea when one hears the tinkle, but one merely sees—well! One sees life at the Front; one hears the roar of the guns; and if one cares to lift one's eyes to the sky one sees copious observation balloons and aeroplanes. The day is very near now. This will probably be my last letter before going into action, so do not worry if you do not hear again for a week.

Cheer up—all's well that ends well!

And in a P.S. I said, "I cannot guarantee even field-cards regularly."

My diary tells the story of these last days until I packed it up with my kit which I handed in when we reached our concentration area in front of the Café Belge on the right of the Vlamertinghe-Ypres road on July 29.

JULY 25TH. We marched off from Watou at 9.30 p.m. We got along very slowly; the North Lancs in front kept halting. However, it was a nice cool evening. We got to Query Camp at 1 a.m. We had dinner and then went to bed in tents at 2.20. Allen and I have a tent to ourselves.

JULY 26TH. Breakfast in bed. Up 10.30. At 11.30 Beesley, Telfer, Sergeant Donovan and I went to the 39th Division Headquarters in C Camp in a wood near by. We saw Major-General Cuthbert while we were there. We were sent to the 39th Division model of the Ypres battlefield where we discussed the operations with the officers of the 1/6th Cheshires on our left. We got back at 1.30 p.m. and had lunch.... Took the afternoon easy; studied maps, etc.... To bed 9.30.

JULY 27TH. Inspections and explanation of scheme in the morning. In the afternoon I went, with Sergeant Baldwin, to reconnoitre the trench on the right of the main road between Vlamertinghe and Ypres, where we are to spend 'XY night'! It was a very hot day. Coming back we (and also Sergeant-Major Preston) got a lorry all the way to Brandhoek. I got back at 4 p. m.... I wrote two or three letters and then had dinner. To bed at 9.30. At 10.15 a zeppelin came over and dropped a big bomb a few hundred yards away, causing a loud explosion. We got up and stood outside the tents looking for the zeppelin; but we could not see it, although there were a whole crowd of search-lights trying to get on to it."

JULY 28TH. Up 8 a.m. Parade 9 a.m. Drill and explanation of campaign. At 12 noon, Major Brighten lectured all officers and N. C. O.'s on the forthcoming battle. He closed with an eloquent peroration in which he said that, although our little bit is only part of very large operations, our holding the Gravenstafel Ridge may help to end the war and sway the destiny of the world! In the afternoon I went into Poperinghe. It was extremely hot. I had a cold bath at the Divisional Baths and felt very refreshed by it. I met Gaulter of the King's Own on the same job. He said that he was not looking forward to the push. His battalion are at present in camp near Poperinghe Station. In the push they will be the right rear battalion of Stockwell's Brigade. After my bath I made one or two purchases in Poperinghe and then had tea there. Having had tea, I returned to Query Camp—by lorry most of the way—where I arrived at 6.30 p.m.

JULY 29TH (SUNDAY). Up 9 a.m. At 10 it poured with rain and prevented Church parade. At 10.30 Allen and I set off with Sergeant Baldwin, Sergeant Donovan, Sergeant Brogden, and a few other N. C. O.'s and runners, to reconnoitre a track. We went on a miniature train as far as Vlamertinghe. Then we walked across the fields. We were in a hot-bed of artillery batteries. Suddenly a shell dropped close to us. Three of our party were wounded—Sergeant Donovan, Lance-Corporal Segar and Private Hampson. Lance-Corporal Segar had a large slice out of his hip, but only a flesh wound, a nice, but painful, 'Blighty'! Donovan and Hampson had slight wounds; they were 'walking cases,' but it will be hospital for them all right. When they were dressed we left them with an R.F.A. man to be taken on the first ambulance; and we then carried on along Track 6, past Salvation Corner, beyond Ypres and into Liverpool Trench. We left some sign-posts there and then walked back to the miniature railway. It was a horribly dirty trip; all the ground was thick with slush. We got a train part of the way back and travelled on an engine the remainder! It was 4.15 p.m. when we got back. We had some tea. Then we attended a conference, presided over by Colonel Best-Dunkley, in Headquarters Mess Hut, to have our last corporate discussion upon the coming battle. There were officers from other units connected with us there; and Best-Dunkley made sure that everybody knew exactly what he had got to do and what assistance he could expect from anybody else. He was calm and dignified and even polite. He concluded the proceedings by making a soldierly appeal to the honour of the battalion, said that he knew that every gentleman in the 2/5th Lancashire Fusiliers would do his duty, that he placed entire confidence in our loyalty and our ability; and remarked that he would not hesitate to recommend for decorations anybody who carried on when wounded or distinguished himself by any conspicuous act of bravery.

Major Brighten looked into our mess tent just before dinner. I was alone, looking at maps. He said that he wondered what I would think of it all when I saw the coming battle in full swing. He told me that the landing on the Coast is not, he thinks, after all, coming off this time! In fact Rawlinson's Fourth Army is not to be in it at all. I expect the German thrust at Nieuport has spoilt Haig's plans there. I am very sorry indeed. Major Brighten said that the plan is completely changed. This battle is going to be fought north and south of Ypres with the object of breaking through here. One would naturally assume so from the number of maps with which we have been issued. Major Brighten is going down to the Transport. He will not take part in this battle unless required. He is on 'battle reserve'; and so are Barlow and Smith as they have arrived so recently, and have not practised the 'stunt.' Harwood is liaison officer with the 1/6th Cheshires on our left.

A and B Companies had a very lively time at dinner this 'X' evening. West was acting the fool and making us all laugh.

At 9.30 p.m. the Battalion left Query Camp and we marched to our concentration trenches beyond Vlamertinghe. The men filed into these trenches—5 and 8 platoons in the same trench. Battalion Headquarters are at Café Belge on the left of the main road. B Company Headquarters are in the cellar of the next cottage on the left. About a hundred yards further on—on the left of the road—is the trench my (8) platoon is in. The organization of my platoon is as follows: Sergeant Baldwin is platoon sergeant, and Corporal Livesey is next in seniority after him. I have five sections. The Bombing Section, under Livesey, consists of eight all told; Tipping's Riflemen, thirteen; Heap's Rifle-Grenade men, eleven; two Lewis Gun Sections—Topping and Hopkinson being the respective section commanders and each having seven in their sections.

Various articles were drawn from a dump when we got to the trench. We got to the trench about 11 p.m.

There my diary of the period abruptly closes. For the events which followed it is necessary to turn to the long letter describing the whole operations which I wrote home from Worsley Hall a few days later. That letter describes the Third Battle of Ypres which is the subject of the next chapter.

CHAPTER 16

The Battle Of Ypres

(July 31st, 1917)

'Tis Zero! Full of all the thoughts of years!
A moment pregnant with a life-time's fears
That rise to jeer and laugh, and mock awhile
The vaunted courage of the human frame,
Till Duty calls, till Love and beck'ning
Fame

Lead forth the heroes to that frenzied line.
The creeping death that, searching, never stays;
To brave the rattling, hissing streams of lead,
The bursting shrapnel and the million ways
That war entices death; when dying, dead
And living, mingle in the ghastly glare
That taints the beauty of a night once fair,
And seems to flout the Majesty divine.

F. Shuker (Zero)

Safely ensconced beneath the sheets of a very comfortable hospital bed at Worsley Hall, I wrote the following letter in which I described the Third Battle of Ypres up to the time when I left the battlefield. For the progress of the battle beyond that it will be necessary to quote other documents. Here is my own account of the operations:

AUGUST 3RD. I will now endeavour to tell you the story of the Third Battle of Ypres. As you are aware, we were preparing for this battle the whole time I was at the Front. It was part of Haig's general plan of campaign for 1917. When I first arrived in the Prison at Ypres, the day before Messines, Captain Andrews had me in his cell and explained to me the plan of campaign.

He opened some maps and explained to me that Plumer's Second Army was, very shortly, going to attack on the south of the Ypres Salient with the object of taking Hill 60 and the Messines Ridge. If that attack should prove successful we should, a few days afterwards, do a little 'stunt' on a German trench named Ice Trench. We were issued with photograph maps of this trench and many conferences were held with regard to it. Further, he explained that this was only a preliminary operation: the main campaign of the year was to be fought on the front between Ypres and the Sea, and Sir Hubert Gough was coming to Ypres to take command.

Well, the Battle of Messines was fought the following morning; all Plumer's objectives were gained; it was a perfect 'stunt'; but, still, our Ice Trench affair was cancelled! We left Ypres soon afterwards and went into rest billets at Millain and then training billets at Westbecourt. Hunter-Weston's VIII Corps became a reserve corps behind the line and we, Jeudwine's 55th Division, were transferred to Watts's XIX Corps which became part of Gough's Fifth Army—that famous general having arrived in Flanders. While at Westbecourt we—Stockwell's 164 Brigade—practised the Third Battle of Ypres in the open cornfields and amongst the numerous vegetable crops between Cormette and Boisdinghem.

When we got back to the Salient we understood Haig's plan to be that Gough's Army should smash forward from Ypres, that there should be a French Army on Gough's left, and that Rawlinson's Fourth Army should land upon, or push up, the Belgian Coast at precisely the same moment as Gough struck north from the Ypres Salient. That plan commended itself to me as highly satisfactory. But one always has to reckon with an enemy as well! I do not know whether Armin got wind of it or not, but he effectively thwarted Haig by doing precisely the kind of thing I expected he would do. Rawlinson's Army was engaged and driven back at Nieuport, thus disorganizing his plans; and Ypres—the other flank—was intensely bombarded with high explosives and gas shells on that never-to-be-forgotten night of July 12-13.

The gas casualties in Ypres who were taken to hospital on July 13 were, I was told, 3,000! A much higher figure than I thought at first. A day or two after these events Gratton came in to us at the Ramparts and casually informed us that the Coast idea was postponed: the battle was going to be fought north and south of Ypres only. The Coast landing was going to take place later if the Third Battle of Ypres should prove a success—of which, of course, no patriot could entertain any doubts! Rawlinson was not ready. Nieuport was to me sufficient explanation for that. And Beatty was not ready! That I do not understand. I was very disappointed, indeed, when I heard this news, as I was not very hopeful as to the chance of success in any battle fought in the centre. A flanking movement is, in my opinion, the best policy; and the original idea would have meant, if a landing had been effected, a triangular advance which would have left before Armin only two alternatives—retreat or surrender. But attrition seems to be far more in Robertson's line than strategy! So the Third Battle of Ypres has begun. And, unless things change very quickly, I am bound to say that it is not a success. So much for the general idea.

During our twenty days in the Ypres Salient, from July 1 to July 20, we suffered very heavily in casualties; and when we came out we were certainly not strong enough to go into battle. So while we were at Valley Camp, Watou, we were reinforced by large drafts. And, in accordance with the above plans, we left Watou on the night of July 25 and marched to Query Camp, near Brandhoek, but on the left of the main road. Here we remained awaiting 'XY night.' 'Z day' was the day on which the battle was to take place.

On 'XY night' we left Query Camp and took up our positions in our concentration trenches near Vlamertinghe. My platoon and Allen's platoon were in a trench on the right of the Vlamertinghe-Ypres road, across the field stretching from the road to the railway. Sergeant Brogden's platoon (6 Platoon) was a little further on. Dickinson was in command of B Company. We had our Headquarters in a little wooden dug-out in the centre of the field behind the trench. Battalion Headquarters were at the Café Belge—a house on the right of the road close by. 'XY night' was the night of July 29-30. We got a little sleep during the morning.

For the last fortnight the artillery had been preparing the way for us, raids had been taking place, and conflicts in the air had been of frequent occurrence; the Royal Engineers had been constructing roads and other means of advance; miniature railways were running up to the front line; and the road from Watou, through Poperinghe and Vlamertinghe, to Ypres was simply thronged with transport. The weather had been fine and hot. On 'XY night' troops were swarming round Vlamertinghe and there was every sign that a great push was about to commence.

During July 30, in our little wooden dug-out here, Dickinson held conferences consisting of Allen and myself with Sergeant Brogden, Sergeant Baldwin, Sergeants Stokes and, of course, Sergeant-Major Preston and Quartermaster-Sergeant Jack. Did it occur to us that within twenty-four hours we should all be scattered to the winds—some killed, others wounded? I expect it did. But it did not worry us. We smiled and discussed plans. During the day Colonel Best-Dunkley looked in and chatted most agreeably; he was in a most friendly mood. Padre Newman also looked in.

At 8.55 p.m. I marched off with my platoon along Track 1. All units were moving up to the line. After I had been going about a quarter of an hour half a dozen shells burst quite close to us, badly putting the wind up us. We all lay on the ground. When the disturbance had subsided we moved on again along Track 1, leaving Goldfish Château, the one building in that region which stands intact, on our right, along Track 6, touching Ypres at Salvation Corner, along the Canal Bank, again across the open and though La Brique, where the Tanks (commanded by Major Inglis) were congregating ready to go forward on the morrow, to Liverpool Trench.

We reached Liverpool Trench, the assembly trench from which we were to go over the top on the morrow, about 11 p. m.... D and B Companies were in Liverpool Trench, and C and A Companies in Congreve Walk—the other side of Garden Street. It was a dull, cloudy night. The guns were continually booming. Our howitzers were flinging gas-shells on to every known German battery throughout the night.

The enemy replied by shelling Liverpool Trench and Congreve Walk—especially the latter. One shell burst right in the trench, took one of Verity's legs almost clean off, and killed his servant Butterworth. The shells were bursting all night. All our trenches were simply packed with troops ready to go over the top at Zero. Lewis's 166 Brigade filled the trenches in front of us. The 55th Division occupied a front from the west of Wieltje to Warwick Farm. Half of this frontage was occupied by Lewis's 166 Brigade on the left, and Boyd-Moss's 165

Brigade occupied the other half on the right. Stockwell's 164 Brigade occupied the whole frontage in rear with the object of passing through the front brigades and penetrating into the enemy's positions.

The 2/5th Lancashire Fusiliers were the left front battalion of the 164 Brigade. Colonel Hindle's 1/4th North Lancashires were on the right. We were supported by the Liverpool Irish as 'moppers up'; and the North Lancs. were supported by the 1/4th King's Own Royal Lancaster Regiment in the same way. In our battalion, D Company, commanded by Captain Bodington, were on the left front. On their right were C Company, commanded by Captain Mordecai. In rear of D Company were B Company commanded by Second-Lieutenant Talbot Dickinson, M.C.; and on our right were A Company commanded by Captain Briggs.

The front companies comprised the first two waves; the rear companies the third and fourth waves. The first wave of D Company contained Beesley's platoon on the left; and behind Beesley's platoon was that of Telfer. Then came Sergeant Brogden's platoon of B Company, with Allen on his right. My platoon occupied the whole Company front behind Brogden and Allen. My orders were to advance to the 'Green Line,' and when I got there I was to take Lance-Corporal Tipping's rifle section and four Lewis Gunners on to reinforce Allen at Aviatick Farm where he was to dig a strong point in front of the front-line when the Gravenstafel Ridge was reached.

Two of my sections were detached: Corporal Livesey took his bombers with Brogden's platoon to mop up a dug-out beyond Wurst Farm, and Lance-Corporal Heap was sent with his rifle grenadiers to 15 Platoon. On my left was a platoon, commanded by Sergeant Whalley, of the 1/6th Cheshires. They belonged to the 118th Brigade of the 39th Division of Maxse's XVIII Corps—so,

153

you see, I was on the extreme left of Sir Herbert Watts's XIX Corps. It was Cuthbert's 39th Division that was to take St. Julien. We were to go through Fortuin and leave St. Julien just on our left. On the right of our division was the 15th Division. Behind us, in the Watou area, was Nugent's 36th (Ulster) Division, ready to go through us in a day or two. The 15th Division is entirely Scottish. So much for Gough's dispositions for the battle.

Zero was fixed for 3.50 in the morning. As the moment drew near how eagerly we awaited it! At 3.50 exactly I heard a mine go up, felt a slight vibration, and, as I rushed out of the little dug-out in which I had been resting, every gun for miles burst forth. What a sight! What a row! The early morning darkness was lit up by the flashes of thousands of guns, the air whistling and echoing with shells, the calm atmosphere shaken by a racket such as nobody who has not heard it could imagine! The weird ruins of Ypres towered fantastically amongst the flashes behind us. In every direction one looked guns were firing. In front of us the 166th and 165th Brigades were dashing across no man's land, sweeping into the enemy trenches, the barrage creeping before them. I stood on the parados of Liverpool Trench and watched with amazement. It was a dramatic scene such as no artist could paint.

Before the battle had been raging half an hour German prisoners were streaming down, only too glad to get out of range of their own guns! I saw half a dozen at the corner of Liverpool Trench and Garden Street. They seemed very happy trying to converse with us. One of them—a boy about twenty—asked me the nearest way to the station; he wanted to get to England as soon as possible!

The Tanks went over. As daylight came on the battle raged furiously. Our troops were still advancing. Messages soon came through that St. Julien had been taken.

Our time was drawing near. At 8.30 we were to go over. At 8 we were all 'standing to' behind the parapet waiting to go over. Colonel Best-Dunkley came walking along the line, his face lit up by smiles more pleasant than I have ever seen before. 'Good morning, Floyd; best of luck!' was the greeting he accorded me as he passed; and I, of course, returned the good wishes. At about 8.20 Captain Andrews went past me and wished me good luck; and he then climbed over the parapet to reconnoitre.

The minutes passed by. Everybody was wishing everybody else good luck, and many were the hopes of 'Blighty' entertained—not all to be realized. It is a wonderful sensation—counting the minutes on one's wrist watch as the moment to go over draws nigh. The fingers on my watch pointed to 8.30, but the first wave of D Company had not gone over. I do not know what caused the delay. Anyhow, they were climbing over. Eventually, at 8.40, I got a signal from Dickinson to go on. So forward we went, platoons in column of route. Could you possibly imagine what it was like? Shells were bursting everywhere. It was useless to take any notice where they were falling, because they were falling all round; they could not be dodged; one had to take one's chance: merely go forward and leave one's fate to destiny.

Thus we advanced, amidst shot and shell, over fields, trenches, wire, fortifications, roads, ditches and streams which were simply churned out of all recognition by shell-fire. The field was strewn with wreckage, with the mangled remains of men and horses lying all over in a most ghastly fashion—just like any other battlefield I suppose. Many brave Scottish soldiers were to be seen dead in kneeling positions, killed just as they were firing on the enemy. Some German trenches were lined with German dead in that position. It was hell and slaughter. On we went. About a hundred yards on my right,

155

slightly in front, I saw Colonel Best-Dunkley complacently advancing, with a walking stick in his hand, as calmly as if he were walking across a parade ground. I afterwards heard that when all C Company officers were knocked out he took command in person of that Company in the extreme forward line. He was still going strong last I heard of him.

We passed through the 166th Brigade. We left St. Julien close on our left. Suddenly we were rained with bullets from rifles and machine-guns. We extended. Men were being hit everywhere. My servant, Critchley, was the first in my platoon to be hit. We lay down flat for a while, as it was impossible for anyone to survive standing up.

Then I determined to go forward. It was no use sticking here for ever, and we would be wanted further on; so we might as well try and dash through it. 'Come along—advance!' I shouted, and leapt forward. I was just stepping over some barbed wire defences—I think it must have been in front of Schuler Farm (though we had studied the map so thoroughly beforehand, it was impossible to recognize anything in this chaos) when the inevitable happened. I felt a sharp sting through my leg. I was hit by a bullet. So I dashed to the nearest shell-hole which, fortunately, was a very large one, and got my first field dressing on. Some one helped me with it. Then they went on, as they were, to their great regret, not hit!

My platoon seemed to have vanished just before I was hit. Whether they were in shell-holes or whether they were all hit, or whether they had found some passage through the wire, I cannot say. I only know that, with the exception of Corporal Hopkinson and one or two Lewis Gunners who went forward soon after, they had all vanished. It was one of the many mysteries of a modern battlefield! Allen was going on all right: I saw him going on in front: I believe he got to Aviatik Farm! It was 10.20 a.m. when I was wounded. I lay in this shell-hole for some time. When I had been there about half an hour the enemy put down a barrage just on the line which contained my shell-hole! It was horrible. I thought I was lost this time. Shells were bursting all around me, making a horrible row; some of them were almost in the trench. I was covered with the fumes from one or two of them and also sniffed some gas. I put on my box-respirator. One piece of shrapnel hit me on the head, but, fortunately, I had my steel helmet on my head; so I was all right.

At 11.30 a.m. I decided that I might just as well be blown to bits in the open, trying to get back to safety, as lying in this shell-hole; so I made a dash for it and got out of the barrage. I inquired the way to the nearest aid post, and was told that it was a long way off. But I proceeded in the direction indicated. Before long I met Corporal Livesey returning from his bombing stunt with about half a dozen prisoners and a shrapnel wound in his back; also another lance-corporal, from D Company, who had been on a similar stunt and was wounded in the ear by a bullet. Some of the prisoners were also wounded. So we all walked down together.

Corporal Livesey told me that Sergeant Brogden was wounded in the arm, Sergeant Stokes killed, and Corporal Chamley wounded. We saw some horrible sights all the way along. We were joined by more prisoners as we went down. German prisoners have only to be told which way to go and they go. They are quite sociable people too—many of them bright-eyed boys of seventeen and eighteen. They are only too glad to carry our wounded men back; they need no escort. We got on very well indeed with them. I suppose that in a sense we were comrades in distress, or, rather comrades in good fortune, in that we were all leaving the field of horrors behind us!

Yet they were the very Boches who, an hour before, had been peppering us with those bullets. One would never have imagined that we had so recently been enemies. One of them asked for water to 'drinken;' so I let him have a drink from my water-bottle. About half a dozen of them drank, and they appeared very grateful.

Germans are not half so vile as they are painted.... They are only doing their bit for their Empire as we are for ours. The pity of it is that destiny should have thrown us into conflict. It is a great pity. How fine it would be if we could let bygones be bygones, shake hands, and lead the world in peace and civilization side by side! If we can fraternize so speedily on the battlefield, why cannot those who are not shooting each other also fraternize? It is a cruel insult to humanity that this thing should go on. War is hell, and the sooner some one arises who has the courage to stop it the better. Somebody will have to take the lead some time.

I myself believe in peace after victory—but we are not yet going the right way about achieving victory; and, unless Sir William Robertson speedily changes his plans, we might as well make peace. This killing business is horrible. The present policy of the General Staff is: see which side can do the most killing. A far wiser, and far more humane, policy would be to win it by strategy. I believe in out-manoeuvring the enemy and taking as many prisoners as possible; make him evacuate territory or surrender by corps and armies; it can be done if we go the right way about it, but this bloodshed is barbarous.

When we walked over Wieltje we found our once 'strong point' no longer existent. The sandbags were scattered all over. Yet in the mine below—in the es-tam—General Stockwell had his Headquarters.

We were sent on from aid-post to aid-post. They were all crowded with wounded. The number of 'walking cases' was very large. At Potijze we were again sent on. So I walked into Ypres and passed the Cathedral and the Cloth Hall and reached the remains of the Prison which is now the central aid-post for Ypres. There was a pleasant padre there; and he got me a refreshing cup of tea.

Then I went on again. I got on a lorry and was taken to the mill at Vlamertinghe, which is known as the 2/1 Wessex Dressing Station. When I got there I was sent upstairs for some tea. On entering the mess, I found Lieutenant Francis also there, having tea. He was wounded in the arm. His arm was in a sling. There were also two or three German officers having tea there. They were quite as sociable as our Allies! Who should come in to see us, a few minutes later, but Major Brighten, who, being on 'battle reserve,' was down at the Transport! He expressed surprise when he saw me, and asked me to tell him all about it. He would insist on carrying some of my equipment downstairs. He informed me that my batman, Critchley, was down below. So I went and saw him. He had got one in the leg too.

I had my wound dressed here and also had an anti-tetanus inoculation put into me. I did not like it!

Then Francis and I got into a motor-ambulance and were motored away, through Poperinghe, to Watou. We passed what I assumed to be Nugent's 36th Division coming up in motor-lorries to relieve the 55th Division. At Watou we were taken to the 10th C.C.S. We had our wounds dressed again there and then had tea. Then we got on to a hospital train which was standing in the siding. Who should join us in the saloon on this train but Gaulter, of the King's Own! He, too, had got one in the leg! The question which interested us most on the way back was whether we would get to 'Blighty.' The train went very slowly. We were held up because the Germans were shelling Hazebrouck of all places. They must have some long-range guns!

We arrived in Boulogne at 5.30 on Wednesday morning, August 1, and were immediately motored to Wimereux, where we entered the 14th General Hospital. We went to bed at once and remained in bed all day and night.

The next morning I was awakened by the greeting: 'You're for England; you leave at 8.15.' So I got up and had breakfast. Then we were motored down to Boulogne again where we all embarked on the St. David, and sailed for the shores of old England. It was a happy voyage. We landed at Dover at midday....

The train left Dover at 4.30 p.m. We reached Manchester at midnight and I and seven others were immediately motored to Worsley. So here I am in a nice cosy bed in the spacious mansion of the Egertons of Ellesmere—Worsley Hall. What vicissitudes one does go through!

So, as far as the writer of this book was concerned, Ypres and all that its name implies was now but a memory: I was safely back on the right side of the water once again. My feelings on leaving "Wipers" behind me can best be expressed in the words which a poet of the 55th Division dedicated to the British Soldier in the second number of *Sub Rosa*:

Good-bye, Wipers! though I 'opes it is for good,
It 'urts me for to leave yer—I little thought it would.

When I gets back to Blighty, and all the fightin's done,
Mebbe the picters of the past will rise up, one by one.

Like movies at the Cinema, they'll bob up in my brain,
The places that I knew so well—I'll see them all again.

The battered-in Asylum; the Prison scorched and scarred;
And 'ole Salvation Corner with the guns a bellowin' 'ard.

The muddy, ruddy, Ramparts; the mist upon the Moat;

The grey Canal between whose banks no barges ever float.
An' them Cathedral ruins—O Gawd, the fearsome sight!
Like mutilated fingers they points up through the night.
The blighters what relieves us—we'll treat 'em fair an' kind,
They're welcome to the soveneers what we 'ave left be'ind.
Good-bye, Wipers! though I 'opes it is for good,
It 'urts me for to leave yer—I little thought it would.

It was with a thrill of pride that I read in the newspapers during the following days of the magnificent achievement of the 55th Division—of the "Lancashire Men's Great Fight:" "Stubborn in attack and withdrawal." I read of heroic fights round Pommern Castle, of Wurst Farm being captured by a gallant young officer, and, particularly, the case of: "An officer who was left last out of his battalion to hold out in an advanced position (who) said to the padre who has just visited him in hospital, 'I hope the General was not disappointed with us.'" The General, I am sure, was not disappointed with these Lancashire men. No one could think of them without enthusiasm and tenderness, marvelling at their spirit and at the fight they made in the tragic hours—because it was a tragedy to them that, after gaining all the ground they had been asked to take, and not easily nor without losses, they should have to fall back and fight severe rear-guard actions to cover a necessary withdrawal.

It was, naturally, a matter of great interest to me to determine to what particular officers these remarks referred, as no names were given and no battalions mentioned by name. Now, of course, we all know. The officer who reached Wurst Farm was John Redner Bodington, and the gallant young officer who fought like a hound at bay, while wounded over and over again, and hoped that "the General was not disappointed," was none other than Bertram Best-Dunkley. And, as the days rolled by, one familiar name after another was recorded in the casualty lists. It was the bloodiest battle in History; the casualty list which contained my name was the longest I have ever seen in the Times.

I wrote to Sergeant Baldwin for information as to the fate of my platoon, and, some time afterwards, received the following reply:

Ward 24,
Ontario Military Hospital,
Orpington, Kent.
August 15th, 1917
Dear Sir,

I have much pleasure in replying to your letter dated August 5th, 1917. I am very pleased indeed to know that you are safe in 'Blighty.' Well, sir, you ask me where I got to when we went over the top. I think you will remember halting and lying down in no man's land. Well, as I lay there the time seemed to be long; then I got up and went to the front of the platoon to see what had gone wrong.

When I got there I found you had gone on and the remainder of the men had not the sense to follow you. So I led on with the remainder, taking my direction from the compass. I reached the hill and passed Schuler Farm on the right. We started to climb the hill and then a funny thing happened: those already at the top came running back again shouting 'Get back and dig in; they are outflanking us.' I took the warning and retired to a suitable position and got the men digging themselves in. We could see the Boches coming over the ridge like a swarm of bees. When they got nearer we opened machine gun and rifle fire.

All the time this was going on the artillery had ceased firing, and I began to feel a bit downhearted. Then things quietened down a bit; so I told the lads to make a drink of tea for themselves, which they did gladly enough. All the time we could see Fritz preparing for a counter-attack and we knew it had to come. I waited patiently keeping a look-out for them coming. The men were getting knocked out one by one, until I had only five; and the Lewis Gun had got a bullet through its pinion which rendered it useless. Nothing happened until the evening, and then the bombardment started and we knew we had something to put up with.

I sent up an S.O.S. rocket and our artillery opened out, but the shells were dropping short and hitting our men. Then we retired for about fifty yards and took up some shell-holes. I looked round and found all my men had vanished. I was amongst some of the Cams. and Herts. I really did not know what to do. The artillery became more intense and still our shells were dropping short. There was another sergeant out of the Cams. in this shell-hole with a few men; so I told him I would go back and try and get in touch with the artillery.

On my way back I got wounded in the leg, so I rolled into a shell-hole. It began to rain and rained heavily all the night. When day broke I found myself covered with clay and mud, and wet through to the skin. I crawled out and looked about me. It was a quiet morning except for a shell bursting now and again, and I could see some men through my glasses, about a mile away, working on a road. I made my way towards them. How I got there I do not know, for I was more dead than alive. I inquired for the dressing-station, which I found after a long walk. I was sent down to the Base to hospital and was sent to England on August 6.

I am pleased to say that I am feeling much better and my wound is getting on nicely. I hope my letter will find you feeling much better for the rest you have worked so hard for. I saw in the casualty list that the Colonel had died of wounds, the Adjutant killed, Sec.-Lt. Gratton missing, Captain Andrews wounded, and Lt. Telfer missing. I think I have told you all the news you require, and hope you enjoy reading it.

With best wishes,

Yours sincerely,

Robert Charles Baldwin, Sgt.

Sergeant Baldwin was awarded the Military Medal for his services on July 31—August 1, 1917.

Having reproduced the personal narratives of our experiences at Ypres, first by myself and then by my platoon sergeant, it is now desirable to see what happened to the Battalion as a whole. For this it will be necessary to quote the official account in the *Lancashire Fusiliers' Annual*. After mentioning the machine-gun fire which caused me to extend my platoon the account goes on to say:

> This fire was so heavy that it not only inflicted severe casualties, but caused confusion in the shaking out into extended order, and it is to be believed that from this moment the correct formation was never absolutely regained. Machine-gun fire was active chiefly from Wine House, Spree Farm, parts of Capricorn Support and Capricorn Keep, Pond Farm, Hindu Cot and other points. Seeing that they could not advance till these points were dealt with, the commanders of the leading waves took steps to take the first points, such as Wine House, Spree Farm, Capricorn Support. These were dealt with at considerable loss, some enemy being captured, some killed and some running away. It was difficult to obtain a definite account of all the incidents that happened before the Black Line was reached, but great gallantry was shown by the officers and N. C. O.'s in rallying and leading the men in face of heavy fire. The Commanding Officer, Lieut.-Colonel B. Best-Dunkley, put himself at the head of all men in his immediate vicinity, and led them on through intense machine-gun fire. Ultimately the Black Line was reached. The casualties up to this point may be

estimated at anything up to 50 per cent of the total strength of the Battalion. However, the advance had to continue and that quickly, as it was impossible to wait to reorganize under the heavy fire; moreover, the advance was timed to a programme of artillery. The advance to the Green Line, the Gravenstafel Switch, 6,000 yards from our original front line, therefore continued. Few details necessarily are obtainable owing to the heavy casualties. The creeping barrage, not a heavy one, certainly not sufficient to deal with the country up to the Green Line, had run away from us. Many more casualties were suffered, but the Battalion eventually reached its objective. Digging in and consolidation at once commenced. Captain J. R. Bodington, commanding left Company, reached Wurst Farm with ten men, this number being shortly reduced by casualties to two. The Green Line had only been in our possession for about twenty minutes when the first enemy counter-attack, consisting of two companies, commenced. This came from a north-easterly direction, sweeping across the front of the division on our left. It was very determined, as the division on our left had not been able to get up; our left flank was quite unprotected.

"An attempt was therefore made to form a defensive flank. The counter-attack halted on a road running north-west and south-east. Finding we had not sufficient men to form a defensive flank, a further withdrawal was ordered to Jew Hill, east of St. Julien. From this point a large enemy counter-attack was observed commencing. This also came from a north-easterly direction, and was apparently simultaneous with that from the south-east affecting the 1/4th Loyal North Lancs.—the battalion on our right. This counter-attack was overwhelming in its strength. It had been preceded by four enemy aircraft, flying low over our advanced positions and firing Véry lights and machine-guns. The lights were apparently the call for artillery cooperation. They were answered by the opening of fire by heavy guns which dealt with individual points. Owing to the general disorganization caused by the very heavy casualties, troops on the whole front of this unit had now to commence a general withdrawal. Isolated points, however, held out most gallantly and held up the advance of the enemy while consolidation on or about the Black Line was completed by troops in rear and whilst the withdrawal of the remainder was safely effected. A small strong point situated west of Schuler Farm was held by one hundred and thirty men of this Battalion, and the 1/8 (Irish) Battalion, King's Liverpool Regiment and with them Captain Bodington, one of the few remaining officers of the Battalion. Those were first attacked from the front, which attack they warded off. The enemy counter-attack then developed on their left and right; both these attacks also were held off for some time by machine-gun, Lewis gun, and rifle fire. The few survivors were forced to withdraw and fight their way back, Captain Bodington and ten other ranks reaching the Black Line safely.

Battalion Headquarters was situated at Spree Farm, and they only received late warning that the enemy were near them. Lieutenant-Colonel B. Best-Dunkley gathered together all men available, and, placing himself at the head, beat off the counter-attack at this point. At this time our own artillery brought down an extremely heavy barrage on the enemy which appeared to catch him, and it was probably due to this that they were unable to gain a footing in the Black Line on our immediate front. During this withdrawal the Adjutant—Lieutenant R. Andrews—was killed. The Commanding Officer was wounded shortly afterwards—about 8 p.m. There was then no officer of this Battalion known to be alive, and the Orderly Room Sergeant—Sergeant F. Howarth—took command, organizing the defence of that part of the line until the Battalion was withdrawn to Bilge Trench, about 9 a.m. the following morning—August 1. Captain Bodington, who was the one surviving officer, came in subsequently from the left of the line.

Let us now follow the movements of Captain Bodington. He afterwards wrote the following report:

Up to the time of reaching a point a hundred yards in rear of the Black Line, the advance was easy.

On crossing the small rise behind Wine House we came under very heavy machine-gun and rifle fire from both Wine House and Spree Farm. Two platoons had to be used in driving the enemy from the above-named farms, and the casualties were heavy in this minor operation.

Both the dug-outs at Wine House and Spree Farm were in fairly good condition, and from here with the remainder of the men we pushed forward towards Border House without much difficulty, and hence to Winnipeg, where we got into touch with the 1/6th Cheshires on our left, and proceeded to the Gravenstafel Ridge. Being left here with only two of my men, I could do no more than reconnoitre Wurst Farm and Aviatik Farm.

Both the dug-outs and O.P. in these farms were in fairly good condition, but must have been evacuated hurriedly, although no documents of any importance could be found.

We could see at a distance of about six hundred yards more of our troops on the right, but unable to get into touch with them as the enemy held posts between us.

On returning to the 1/6th Cheshires on our left, a counter-attack had already been launched against their left flank, consequently it was decided to withdraw to the Winnipeg-Kansas Cross Roads. It was found impossible to make a stand here, so the withdrawal continued to a point where the 13th Sussex Regiment had dug themselves in on Jew Hill.

About two hours elapsed, when it was found that a party of the enemy were getting round their left flank. A party was at once detailed to deal with this, but at this time I became detached from this party and consequently reported back to Battalion Headquarters, then situated at Spree Farm.

I was at once detailed to take a party up to reinforce a partly organized strong point about the dug-outs at D. 13. a. 8.0. I found here two officers and about one hundred men. The position was strong, but both flanks were unguarded.

There were two machine-guns and one Lewis gun. After a short time a strong counter-attack was made by the enemy on this position from the front which was easily beaten off, but almost simultaneously we were attacked on either flank.

By this time, another machine-gun had been brought into position, but the Lewis gun had used up all its magazines. A number of casualties had been caused. We held the enemy for half an hour, and a heavy battery was shelling us considerably. Two direct hits were obtained causing a number of casualties. Meanwhile the enemy was advancing on either flank. It was found that only forty or fifty men remained, and little means of escape was left, but it was decided to withdraw to a line well wired about three hundred yards in rear. On reaching this point it was found to be untenable and the withdrawal continued to the Black Line, where some of the 165 and 166 Brigades had been digging in.

They were at once warned of the advance of the enemy, and here he was finally beaten off. A number of casualties were sustained in the withdrawal from the dug-outs behind Schuler Farm. At that time we could not get into touch on our left, but the gap was soon filled in by a party of the 6th King's Liverpool Regiment and the Battalion Headquarters from Spree Farm. Later we got into touch with the 1/5th South Lancashire Regiment on our left and the 45 Brigade on our right.

At that time I could find none of my own Battalion.
(Signed) *J. R. Bodington*,
Captain,
2/5th Battalion Lancashire Fusiliers.

The official chronicler in the *Lancashire Fusiliers' Annual* writes of what remained of the 2/5th Lancashire Fusiliers:

Spent August 1, Minden Day, in the utmost discomfort in Bilge Trench, everybody was soaked through from the pouring rain. However, we all flaunted Minden roses in our helmets. On August 2nd we were relieved and marched back to our transport lines. There all preparations had been made for us and everybody enjoyed a good hot meal. The same evening we were taken back in buses to the Watou area.

It was on July 31 that Philip Cave Humfrey distinguished himself by his able and courageous leading of his Transport to carry supplies to the worn and wearied troops.

He led one hundred pack mules, laden with ammunition and bombs, through heavy enemy barrage to a point close behind our lines which was then being defended against a strong counter-attack. At this point he unloaded his mules in spite of hostile machine-gun and rifle fire, and the ammunition which he brought up was immediately used by the troops who were defending the position. By his promptness and fearlessness he greatly assisted the defence at a critical moment.

For this act of gallantry he was awarded the Military Cross.

Many were the brave deeds done and numerous the honours gained by the officers, non-commissioned officers and men of the Battalion on this historic day. Captain Bodington was awarded the Military Cross as a matter of course. He was the sole combatant officer who came through unscathed, and his unique services have already been fully recorded; he showed himself on July 31, what he has invariably shown himself since, an incomparable man over the top, fearless and ruthless, ever where the fight is hottest and always ready to display his individual initiative on all possible and impossible occasions, a born man of action to whom long experience of shot and shell has made the art of modern war a second nature—an officer after Best-Dunkley's own heart: the Military Cross was the least form of recognition which could reward such an achievement as his.

The bright and chivalrous Newman too—who had already been recommended for the Military Cross for his bravery in tending wounded at the Menin Gate on Messines Night—won this decoration by his unselfish devotion to duty on July 31. Horace Beesley commanded his platoon with such courage and success right out on our far-flung battle line in the vicinity of Wurst Farm and Aviatik Farm until he was badly wounded; and to him also was the Military Cross awarded. And John Agnew, who was second-in-command of C Company, took command of that company when Captain Mordecai was wounded: "Although shot through the knee, he continued to advance and lead his men to their objective—a distance of some 4,000 yards. He was then again wounded and had to return, being wounded a third time on his way back. Although his wounds were serious he refused to take a stretcher, in order that more serious cases might be dealt with. He set a splendid example of pluck and unselfishness."

The Military Cross was also Agnew's reward. When I met him again at Scarborough he was a cripple. Heroic, too, was the end of that flamboyant patriot Talbot Dickinson, M. C., my Company Commander. "He was wounded in the arm," wrote one of his friends, "but carried on to a very advanced position, and, while encouraging his men, was shot through the head." With him Sergeant-Major Preston, too, was killed.

Sergeant Howarth was awarded the Distinguished Conduct Medal for his personal initiative in taking command of the Battalion when no officers were to be found, and for the able way in which he executed his task; and the D. C. M. was also awarded to Lance-Corporal Lawson.

Eleven Military Medals were awarded for deeds done that day: Sergeant Baldwin, Sergeant Olive, Corporal Fox, Lance-Corporal Furnes, Sergeant Hudson, and Privates Baron, Daynes, R. Turner, Rouse, Rodwell and Fitzpatrick.

The casualties, as has already been pointed out, were tremendous. Five hundred and ninety-three other ranks went into battle; four hundred and seventy-three became casualties. It was a very tiny Battalion therefore that went to rest, reorganize, and train at Le Poirier a few days later!

Gilbert Verity had expired shortly after his misfortune in Congreve Walk. Douglas Bernard Priestly was shot through the head and killed instantly almost as soon as he got over the top. The fate of the Adjutant, Reggie Andrews, whom I last saw aimlessly wandering about the battlefield shortly after we went over and who looked over his glasses at me and inquired whether I had seen anything of Headquarters, has already been recorded. And the Assistant-Adjutant met a similar fate: Gratton was, first of all, wounded and he lay in a shell-hole; and while he was in the shell-hole another shell came right into the hole and took his head clean off. Joye remained with Colonel Best-Dunkley until quite late in the day, when he got the 'Blighty' in the leg which was to send him to join me at Worsley Hall.

Captain Briggs, Telfer, and Young, together with a large number of other ranks, were taken prisoners; Briggs and Telfer were also wounded. West was badly wounded. Captain Andrews, Captain Mordecai and Donald Allen were all wounded quite early in the day. Out of nineteen combatant officers eighteen were casualties. The non-combatants, Padre Newman and Dr. Adam came through this battle safely, but they were both wounded at the Battle of Menin Road on September 20! Newman got to England with his wound after that battle, but he was very soon back with the Battalion again to play an even more conspicuous part in the drama of the Great War.

It was a great day was the 31st of July. General Gough sent the following message of congratulation to Brigadier-General Stockwell:

> The Army Commander wishes to convey his thanks and congratulations to the G.O.C. and all ranks of the 164th Infantry Brigade on their fine performance on July 31st. They carried out their task in a most gallant manner and fought splendidly to retain their hold on the ground won.
>
> All officers showed energy, courage, and initiative in dealing with the situation, and the men under their command in spite of heavy losses did their utmost by carrying out their orders to ensure our success and the enemy's defeat. Great credit is due to G. O. C. 164th Brigade for the magnificent behaviour of the troops under his command." And Stockwell sent on the message with the following personal addition:"The Brigadier-General Commanding has much pleasure in forwarding the above remarks of the Army Commander. He considers that all the credit is due to the officers and men of the Brigade.

Major-General Jeudwine congratulated Stockwell in the following terms:

> Well done, 164th Brigade. I am very proud of what you did to-day. It was a fine performance and no fault of yours you could not stay." And in the course of a Special Order of the Day issued to his Division on August 3, General Jeudwine said: "The attack you made on the 31st is worthy to rank with the great deeds of the Brit-

ish Army in the past, and has added fresh glory to the records of that Army.

Meanwhile, the supreme hero of the day lay at the Main Dressing Station mortally wounded. But like Sir Henry Lawrence long ago he had the consolation of feeling that he had tried to do his duty. The Reverend James Odgen Coop, D. S. O., T. D., M. A., the Senior Chaplain to the 55th Division, visited the dying Best-Dunkley at the Main Dressing Station on August 1. It was to Colonel Coop that Colonel Best-Dunkley said that he hoped the General was satisfied, and Colonel Coop recounted the conversation to General Jeudwine. Old "Judy's" heart was touched as it always was by any deeds of gallantry, and to Best-Dunkley he immediately wrote the following historic letter:

Headquarters,
55th Division.
1st August, 1917 (Minden Day).

Dear Best-Dunkley,

The padre has given me your message, and I am very much touched by it.

Disappointed! I should think not, indeed. I am more proud of having you and your Battalion under my command than of anything else that has ever happened to me.

It was a magnificent fight, and your officers and men behaved splendidly, fighting with their heads as well as with the most superb pluck and determination.

The 31st July should for all time be remembered by your Battalion and Regiment and observed with more reverence even than Minden Day. It was no garden of roses that you fought in. I have heard some of the stories of your Battalion's doings and they are glorious. And I have heard of your own doings too, and the close shave you had.

Nothing would give me greater pleasure than that you should come back and command your Battalion, and I greatly hope you will. I am afraid you have painful wounds, but I trust they will not keep you long laid by.

The best of luck to you.

Yours,

H. S. Jeudwine

General Jeudwine's hopes were not to be realized. After a few days' agony Best-Dunkley passed away. On August 6 Major Brighten issued the following pathetic Special Order to the 2/5th Lancashire Fusiliers at Le Poirier:

> I regret to inform all ranks of the Battalion that our late Commanding Officer, Lieut.-Colonel B. Best-Dunkley, died at a C. C. S. yesterday from wounds received in the attack on 31st July—an attack to the magnificent achievement of which he contributed so largely in the long preparation and training and in the actual carrying out. His personal gallantry in leading on the Battalion in the face of heavy enemy fire was an example of bravery and courage which has added to the laurels of the Regiment, and his loss is one which will be felt deeply.
>
> (Signed) *G. S. Brighten,*
>
> Major,
>
> Commanding 2/5 Battalion,
>
> Lancashire Fusiliers.
>
> August 6th, 1917

Best-Dunkley was buried at Proven. The funeral was taken by Padre Newman. As the body was lowered into the Flanders clay General Jeudwine exclaimed: "We are burying one of Britain's bravest soldiers!" The Battalion buglers played the Last Post. And the spot where the hero lies is marked by the traditional Little Wooden Cross.

The crowning triumph came when he was awarded the Victoria Cross; though, to the great sorrow of all, he did not live to know that he had won it. I well remember the excitement in the Mess at "Montpellier" at Scarborough when we read the following announcement in the *Manchester Guardian*:

Capt. (T./Lt.-Col.) Bertram Best-Dunkley
Late Lan. Fus.

For most conspicuous bravery and devotion to duty when in command of his battalion, the leading waves of which, during an attack, became disorganized by reason of rifle and machine-gun fire at close range from positions which were believed to be in our hands. Lieutenant-Colonel Best-Dunkley dashed forward, rallied his leading waves, and personally led them to the assault of these positions, which, despite heavy losses, were carried.

He continued to lead his battalion until all their objectives had been gained. Had it not been for this officer's gallant and determined action it is doubtful if the left of the brigade would have reached its objectives. Later in the day, when our position was threatened, he collected his battalion headquarters, led them to the attack, and beat off the advancing enemy. This gallant officer has since died of wounds.

And some time afterwards I noticed, in an illustrated paper, a little photo entitled "Daddy's V. C." It was the picture of a little baby being held in his mother's arms at Buckingham Palace, while His Majesty King George the Fifth pinned upon his frock the Victoria Cross.

Appendices

APPENDIX 1

Murray and Allenby

In view of my comments upon the appointment of Sir Edmund Allenby to succeed Sir Archibald Murray, the following extract from the Manchester Guardian of September 17, 1919, is of interest:

THE VICTOR AND HIS PREDECESSOR

When Field-Marshal Allenby stepped off the train at Victoria to-day one of the first men whom he greeted was General Sir Archibald Murray, his predecessor in the East. The meeting must have been a pregnant one to them both. Sir Edmund Allenby came home victor of our most successful campaign in the war to receive a peerage, while inside and outside the station London was roaring its welcome. General Murray, after the failure of the battle of Gaza, had been transferred home and had been received there with the severest criticism and some personal attacks. The War Office is famous for its short ways when it does make up its mind to do something disagreeable, and its treatment of Sir Archibald Murray is said to have lacked nothing in discourtesy. Since then a good deal has come out about the early part of our war in the East and the work done by General Murray, and the nearness he got to success with quite inadequate support had become recognized even before Sir Edmund Allenby's dispatch was published, which officially re-established his military reputation.

To-day, at Dover, Sir Edmund Allenby spoke even more clearly of the debt he owed for the foundations laid by General Murray and for the loyal way in which he started him off as a beginner. It is not too common in our military history to find great commanders on the same battle-ground as sensitive about one another's reputation as they are of their own. It is so easy to say nothing and leave matters to history. The lustre of Allenby's achievement is even greater for his acknowledgment of his debt to his predecessor.

THE FIRST PALESTINE CAMPAIGN

Something may be added now about General Murray's work in the East. He commanded in Egypt from January, 1916, to May, 1917. During that time he dealt with the Gallipoli forces, disorganized and with most of their supplies gone. He had to reorganize them into a fighting force again and to send them West. He had to organize and plan the campaign against the Senussi, to be responsible for the internal condition of Egypt, and to defend Egypt from the Turks, then relieved of the Gallipoli operations. The Turkish attack was beaten off and four thousand prisoners taken, the defences of Egypt were pushed forward through the Sinai desert, water-lines carried up and wire ways laid, and all the vast preparations made by which it became possible to take Palestine. His two assaults on Gaza failed, but he held the ground he had taken, including the Wadi Ghuzze, which would have been a big natural defence of Palestine.

He was fighting with three divisions very far short of their full strength and several battalions of dismounted yeomanry, four big guns, and thirty aeroplanes, all of old-fashioned type. His pipe-line was within distance from which it seemed possible to "snap" the Turks at Gaza, but fog delayed the start, and the manoeuvre took too long, and the cavalry fell back from want of water. The snap was so near a success that they picked up a wireless from the Germans in Gaza to their base saying

"Good-bye," as they were going into captivity. That was the main point of the story.

According to General Murray's friends what happened in Palestine was what has happened so often in our history. A general is given a job to do with insufficient forces, and urged on despite his appeals for a sufficient force. He fails. Another commander is appointed, and the new man naturally can exact his own conditions, begins the task with an adequate force, and succeeds. All this, of course, does not take away a single leaf from Sir Edmund Allenby's brilliant boys or suggest that General Murray could have done so well. All that is suggested is that he did not get the same chance.

Appendix 2

The Infantry at Minden

The six Infantry Regiments engaged at Minden, on August 1, 1759, were:

12th Foot—Suffolk Regiment.
20th Foot—Lancashire Fusiliers.
23rd Foot—Royal Welsh Fusiliers.
25th Foot—King's Own Scottish Borderers.
37th Foot—Hampshire Regiment.
51st Foot—King's Own (Yorkshire Light Infantry).

Tradition tells that in the course of the operations at Minden, the 20th were passing through flower gardens and, while doing so, the men plucked some of the roses and wore them in their coats. This story was the origin of the "Minden Rose" which is worn annually, on August 1, by all ranks of the Lancashire Fusiliers.

APPENDIX 3

General Rawlinson and Ostend

Field-Marshal French did not definitely state in his fourth dispatch that General Rawlinson landed at Ostend, but he devoted a number of paragraphs to the subject of "the forces operating in the neighbourhood of Ghent and Antwerp under Lieutenant-General Sir Henry Rawlinson, as the action of his force about this period exercised, in my opinion, a great influence on the course of the subsequent operations." However, in "1914" Lord French has written:

I returned to Abbeville that evening. I found that an officer had arrived from Ostend by motor with a letter from Rawlinson, in which he explained the situation in the north, the details of which we know." And John Buchan in *Nelson's History of the War*, Vol. IV (page 33), states that: "On 6th October the 7th Division began to disembark at Zeebrugge and Ostend, and early on 8th October the former point saw the landing of the 3rd Cavalry Division, after a voyage not free from sensation. The force formed the nucleus of the Fourth Corps, and was commanded by Major-General Sir Henry Rawlinson, who had a long record of Indian, Egyptian, and South African service."

G. H. Perris in The Campaign of 1914 in France and Belgium is even more emphatic: on page 305 of that work he writes: "Part of the 4th British Corps—the 7th Infantry Division and the 3rd Cavalry Division—under Sir Henry Rawlinson, had been landed at Ostend and Zeebrugge without interference, and had advanced eastward to cover the Belgian-British retreat to the south.

Edward III and the Order of the Garter

Colonel Best-Dunkley's question on this subject can best be answered by quoting in full the first paragraph of Chapter XVI of David Hume's History of England, Vol. I:

The prudent conduct and great success of Edward in his foreign wars had excited a strong emulation and a military genius among the English nobility; and these turbulent barons, overawed by the crown, gave now a more useful direction to their ambition, and attached themselves to a prince who led them to the acquisition of riches and glory. That he might further promote the spirit of emulation and obedience, the king instituted the order of the garter, in imitation of some orders of a like nature, religious as well as military, which had been established in different parts of Europe. The number received into this order consisted of twenty-five persons, besides the sovereign; and as it has never been enlarged, this badge of distinction continues as honourable as at its first institution, and is still a valuable, though a cheap present, which the prince can confer on his greatest subjects. A vulgar story prevails, but is not supported by any ancient authority, that at a court ball, Edward's mistress, commonly supposed to have been the Countess of Salisbury, dropped her garter; and the king, taking it up, observed some of the courtiers to smile, as if they thought that he had not obtained this favour merely by accident: upon which he called out, '*Honi soit qui mal y pense*,' Evil to him that evil thinks; and as every incident of gallantry among those ancient warriors was magnified into a matter of great importance, he instituted the order of the garter in memorial of this event, and gave these words as the motto of the order. This origin, though frivolous, is not unsuitable to the manners of the times; and it is indeed difficult by any other means to account, either for the seemingly unmeaning terms of the motto, or for the peculiar badge of the garter, which seems to have no reference to any purpose either of military use or ornament.

Goldfish Château

The following note about Goldfish Château, contained in the Manchester Guardian of September 8, 1919, is relevant to the text:

All the men who had any part in the tragic epic of Ypres will be interested in the news that the Church Army has taken over "Goldfish Château" as a hostel for pilgrims to the illimitable graveyards in the dreadful salient.

For some reason (writes a correspondent who was in it) we christened the place "Goldfish Château." It was a somewhat pretentious mansion, in Continental flamboyant style, standing just off the Vlamertinghe road about half a mile our side of Ypres. Its grounds are ploughed up by shells and bombs, but most of the fountains and wretched garden statuary remains with the fishponds which perhaps gave the villa its army name, and rustic bridges most egregiously incongruous with the surrounding death and desolation.

All through the Ypres fighting it was a conspicuous landmark well known to every soldier, and used, as things got hotter and hotter, as staff headquarters, first for corps, then for division, and finally for brigade and battalion.

Strangely enough, the château never received a direct hit, though all the country round was ploughed up and every other building practically flattened out. The camp tales accounted for this immunity in all sorts of sinister ways. One story was that some big German personage had occupied the place. Probably these were romantic fictions. But the fact remained that "Goldfish Château" bore a charmed life in spite of the fact that the German sausage balloons almost looked down the chimneys and so many staffs lived there. Hundreds of thousands of men in this country who could not name half the county towns in England would be able to describe every room in this Belgian villa outside Ypres. Lancashire soldiers are well acquainted with it.

During the third battle of Ypres the transport of the 55th Division had to leave the fields just opposite the château in a hurry. The Germans not only shelled the place searchingly, but one morning sent over about a dozen bombing planes. Simultaneous shelling and bombing is not good for the nerves of transport mules. But the luck of the "Goldfish Château" held. Nothing hit it.

LEONAUR

ALSO FROM LEONAUR

LEONAUR

ALSO FROM LEONAUR

AVAILABLE IN SOFTCOVER OR HARDCOVER WITH DUST JACKET

CAPTAIN OF THE 95th (Rifles) *by Jonathan Leach*—An officer of Wellington's Sharpshooters during the Peninsular, South of France and Waterloo Campaigns of the Napoleonic Wars.

THE KHAKEE RESSALAH *by Robert Henry Wallace Dunlop*—Service & adventure with the Meerut volunteer horse during the Indian mutiny 1857-1858

BUGLER AND OFFICER OF THE RIFLES *by William Green & Harry Smith* With the 95th (Rifles) during the Peninsular & Waterloo Campaigns of the Napoleonic Wars

BAYONETS, BUGLES AND BONNETS *by James 'Thomas' Todd*—Experiences of hard soldiering with the 71st Foot - the Highland Light Infantry - through many battles of the Napoleonic wars including the Peninsular & Waterloo Campaigns

A NORFOLK SOLDIER IN THE FIRST SIKH WAR *by J W Baldwin*—Experiences of a private of H.M. 9th Regiment of Foot in the battles for the Punjab, India 1845-46

A CAVALRY OFFICER DURING THE SEPOY REVOLT *by A.R.D. Mackenzie*—Experiences with the 3rd Bengal Light Cavalry, the Guides and Sikh Irregular Cavalry from the outbreak to Delhi and Lucknow

THE ADVENTURES OF A LIGHT DRAGOON *by George Farmer & G.R. Gleig*—A cavalryman during the Peninsular & Waterloo Campaigns, in captivity & at the siege of Bhurtpore, India

THE COMPLEAT RIFLEMAN HARRIS *by Benjamin Harris as told to & transcribed by Captain Henry Curling*—The adventures of a soldier of the 95th (Rifles) during the Peninsular Campaign of the Napoleonic Wars

THE RED DRAGOON *by W.J. Adams*—With the 7th Dragoon Guards in the Cape of Good Hope against the Boers & the Kaffir tribes during the 'war of the axe' 1843-48

THE LIFE OF THE REAL BRIGADIER GERARD - Volume 1 - THE YOUNG HUSSAR 1782 - 1807 *by Jean-Baptiste De Marbot*—A French Cavalryman Of the Napoleonic Wars at Marengo, Austerlitz, Jena, Eylau & Friedland

THE LIFE OF THE REAL BRIGADIER GERARD Volume 2 IMPERIAL AIDE-DE-CAMP 1807 - 1811 *by Jean-Baptiste De Marbot*—A French Cavalryman of the Napoleonic Wars at Saragossa, Landshut, Eckmuhl, Ratisbon, Aspern-Essling, Wagram, Busaco & Torres Vedras

Printed in the United Kingdom
by Lightning Source UK Ltd.
131002UK00001B/197/A